Animals and Man
in Historical Perspective

*the text of this book is printed
on 100% recycled paper*

BASIC CONDITIONS OF LIFE

Animals and Man
in Historical Perspective

Edited by
JOSEPH *and* BARRIE KLAITS

 HARPER TORCHBOOKS
Harper & Row, Publishers
New York, Evanston, San Francisco, London

A hardcover edition of this book is published by Harper & Row, Publishers, Inc.

Contents

Acknowledgments

Orest Ranum of Johns Hopkins University first suggested the theme of this book and encouraged us in our unorthodox approach. Among our contributors W. Norman Brown of the University of Pennsylvania and Henri F. Ellenberger of the Université de Montréal offered helpful advice and friendly cooperation. As always, Harry M. Orlinsky of Hebrew Union College–Jewish Institute of Religion was ready to listen and share with us his stimulating erudition. To all these people we extend our warmest thanks.

We thank Philip H. Abelson, editor of *Science,* for granting us permission to reprint the article by Lynn White, Jr. Acknowledgments are also due to the following publishers and other copyright holders: Dover Publications, Inc., the Regents of the University of California, Editions Desclée de Brouwer, Houghton Mifflin Company, James Brown, Inc., J. B. Lippincott Company, Harper & Row, Publishers, Inc., Hutchinson Publishing Group, Ltd., Michael Joseph, Ltd., and St. Martin's Press.

Marian Wilson of Oakland University typed the manuscript with her usual efficient skill, found ways to repair many stylistic blunders in our writing, and enjoyed the project with us.

J. K.
B. K.

Introduction

People love and pity animals; we also use, abuse, and fear them. Animals are our companions, our amusements, and our sustenance. We pursue animals to satisfy our tastes in food and fashion or to enjoy the raw pleasure of destruction. The pursuit can also be creative, as when we seek their images through art and literature. And when we have animals in captivity, we thoroughly scrutinize their appearance, their behavior, and their spirit. Children and adults, in all times and places, in all walks of life, participate in one way or another in the pursuit of animals. What are we really after? Mirrors of ourselves? Alternatives to ourselves? In animals we may discover our kindred spirits, our physical or psychological identities, our moral strengths and weaknesses, and much more. All that is most elusive in man we hope to capture in animals.

The ties between people and animals are as mysterious and as obvious as the mutual devotion of a boy and his dog. We catch glimpses of these ties when we watch a circus parade, when we see someone's pet crushed in an accident, or when we witness the birth of kittens. Exhilaration, compassion, wonder—intangible responses like these are this book's *raisons d'être*.

We have collected a series of readings that attempt to analyze such responses. The writers of the following selections wear many professional hats—biologist, historian, psychiatrist, novelist, and critic. Despite impressive stylistic and substantive differences, these authors share a concern with the issue we have regarded as the leitmotif of this book: What do man's attitudes and behavior toward animals tell us about the historical development of human society and culture? This question immediately suggests a host of more specific problems. How shall we interpret parallels in human and animal behavior? How do religious and other cultural norms shape our attitudes toward animals? How do the changes in the organization of zoos reflect man's altering self-image and his definition of the animal? How do our attitudes toward pets reflect divergent concepts of "civilization"? What is the biological and cultural significance of animal domestication? What are the origins of modern "humanitarian" attitudes toward animals? These are the issues to which the articles in this collection address themselves.

First, what binds us psychologically to animals, especially to the higher vertebrates? Perhaps it is the same condition that binds human beings to each other. Intuitively we recognize our common feelings of fear, hunger, and boredom; our needs to find a mate and a home, to reproduce ourselves, to communicate, and to belong to a society or to something larger than our private selves. Contemporary research on animal behavior has, if anything, blurred the line between man and animals;[1] not that such a line has ever been perfectly clear. Natural historians and philosophers since ancient times have been committed to investigating the relationship between human and subhuman.

1. In the laboratory and in the field, nonhuman primates reveal a range of cognitive abilities as well as emotional experiences and social organizations entirely comparable to our own. See for examples of laboratory work Allan M. Schrier, Harry F. Harlow, Fred Stollnitz, eds., *Behavior of Nonhuman Primates*, 2 vols. (New York, 1965); and Robert M. Yerkes and Ada W. Yerkes, *The Great Apes* (New Haven, 1929). Two celebrated field studies are Jane Van Lawick-Goodall, *In the Shadow of Man* (Boston, 1971); and George B. Schaller, *The Mountain Gorilla* (Chicago, 1963).

The formulation itself suggests a hierarchy, and Aristotle was among the first to designate a chain of being progressing structurally from the simple to the complex, and intellectually from the instinctive to the rational and moral. Aristotle and his successors in the seventeenth and eighteenth centuries devoted great care to the description and classification of animal species. For the ancients, species occupied fixed, eternal positions; and even in the seventeenth century anatomists initiated their investigations within the framework of an immutable Great Chain of Being.[2] Edward Tyson, for instance, set as his goal in 1699 "to enumerate and remark all the different Species, and their Gradual Perfections from one to another." What the anatomists discovered, however, threw this procedure into question. Linnaeus was hard pressed to find generic characters by which to distinguish man from the apes, and in his *System of Nature* (1735) he classified man together with the ape and sloth as a quadruped, in the order *Anthropomorpha*.[3] Travelers to remote corners of the earth brought back accounts of new anthropoid species which the classifiers tried to fit into their schemes. The problems that ensued led Buffon to hesitantly deny in the 1770s that there was anything immutable about existing species; the development of differences among genera, he wrote, was "gradual and marked by minute shades."[4] For the fixed Chain that according to the Christian view ascended from animals through man to the angels and God, eighteenth-century biologists were on the verge of substituting the dynamic concept of evolutionary development.

Within seventy-five years that radical notion became the pre-

2. The classic book on this subject is Arthur O. Lovejoy, *The Great Chain of Being, A Study of the History of an Idea* (Cambridge, Mass., 1936).

3. John C. Greene, *The Death of Adam, Evolution and Its Impact on Western Thought* (1959; reprinted New York, 1961), pp. 178–179.

4. Arthur O. Lovejoy, "Buffon and the Problem of Species," in Bentley Glass, ed., *Forerunners of Darwin: 1745–1859* (Baltimore, 1959), pp. 84–113. The other articles in this volume are also most illuminating.

vailing orthodoxy. Animals and man no longer were conceived as permanent residents of separate compartments of creation. Instead, the evolutionary view, for which Darwin supplied the explanatory mechanism of natural selection, sees time as a moving belt along which species emerge and slowly change into new species.[5] The long-term "Darwinian revolution" in human thought, which in some respects antedates Darwin and in others is not yet completed, regards man and animals as parts of a continuum. Hence, one of the themes of modern ethology (the study of animal behavior) is an effort to illuminate human ways through the study of animals. In the hands of behaviorist psychologists using the artificial environment of the controlled laboratory, this approach can produce a crude reductionism that applies the model of the machine both to man and animals. A far more sophisticated and sensitive procedure is represented by H. Hediger in the first excerpt of this collection. Hediger, director of the Zoological Gardens of Zurich, takes animal behavior as he finds it in the natural habitat and tries to adapt the artificial environment of the zoo to the animals' needs. This procedure requires meticulous observation and cultivated biological empathy analogous to the sensitivity of the ethnographer studying a faraway human society. By asking a few simple but immensely difficult questions about how animals live, Hediger draws parallels between animal and human attitudes toward home or nest, territory, and lines of communication.

The scientist's insight articulates what perhaps has always

5. For Darwin the key to evolution is chance. Fortuitous combinations of environmental conditions determine which organisms will survive to reproduce. Random changes in environment and organic life over time have shaped the picture of the past, and continue to shape the present and future. The combined processes are not so orderly or predictable as to be analyzed in terms of Newtonian mechanics. Darwin's sensitivity to complex historical processes is at the heart of the ongoing "Darwinian revolution." See Loren Eiseley, "The Intellectual Antecedents of *The Descent of Man*," in Bernard Campbell, ed., *Sexual Selection and "The Descent of Man," 1871–1971* (Chicago, 1972).

been the unconscious human perception of kinship with the beasts; concern with animals is an apparently universal human phenomenon. Yet the particular expression of this concern reflects specific cultural patterns. The next two essays in this book, written by distinguished historians of medieval Europe and ancient India, view our attitudes toward animals through a cultural perspective.

In India and the Christian West, argue Lynn White, Jr., and W. Norman Brown, religion remains the primary determinant of human attitudes toward animals. According to White, the assumptions of traditional Christianity pervade our "secular" society. The Judeo-Christian God of our heritage does not dwell in the beasts and land around us; instead, animals and the rest of the natural world were created by Him to serve man's needs. These axioms deprive animals and nature of the exalting, divine status assigned them in animistic or pantheistic religions. Of all the Hebraic creation, only man was made in God's image. Moreover, the God of the Hebrews ordained anthropocentrism when He told Noah after the Flood: "The fear and the dread of you shall be upon all the beasts of the earth and upon all the birds of the sky—everything with which the earth is astir—and upon all the fish of the sea; they are given into your hand."[6]

The immediate context of this bestowal of overlordship seems to be dietary, as the next verse states that "every creature that lives shall be yours to eat." Similarly, the stricture of the Decalogue, "You shall not murder," applied to human victims only; killing animals for consumption and other purposes was entirely permissible. By contrast, in the Hindu, Jain, and Buddhist faiths, the eating of meat signifies an abhorrent violation of Ahinsa, the principle of noninjury to living things. Ahinsa is

---

6. Gen. 9:3. This and subsequent biblical quotations are from the Jewish Publication Society translation, *The Torah: The Five Books of Moses* (Philadelphia, 1962).

an ethical precept derived from the axiom that all life is spiritually continuous and therefore sacred. Logically, although as Brown sees it perhaps not historically, the concept of Ahinsa was reinforced by the doctrine of transmigration of souls. A believer's purely selfish interest would dictate prudence in treatment of animals, since acts in this life determine one's condition in a future existence. Thus, while in Judaism and Christianity there is a sharp line drawn between human and animal, the Indian notion of reincarnation erases this boundary and permits animals the dignified status of once and future men.

The celebrated Hindu doctrine of the sacred cow, a special application of reverence for animals, symbolizes the regard for life in Indian religions. In the Vedic creation myth, an important source for the tradition of cow sanctity, the cosmic waters which give birth to the sun and establish universal law are depicted as pregnant cows. Another important feminine figure of the Veda is Aditi, who has the form of a cow. Aditi gave the initial impulse to create universal order out of chaos and is identified with motherliness and the earth. Thus in Vedic tradition the cow is the symbolic vehicle for the act of creation, the creative and procreative impulse, and the earth itself.[7] It is impossible to imagine a greater contrast to the Hebrew creation myth with its God who created nature, set an unbridgeable gulf between Himself and His creatures, and delegated authority over animals to man.

The two world views are as far apart as East and West, and each hemisphere has its own unique and peculiar moral imperatives. Yet as White and Brown describe heresies or departures

7. W. Norman Brown, "The Sanctity of the Cow in Hinduism," *Journal of the Madras University* 28 (January 1957): 29–49. This has been reprinted twice: (1) *Economic Weekly* (Bombay), Annual Number, February 1964, pp. 245–255; (2) "La vache sacrée dans la religion hindoue," *Annales: économies, sociétés, civilisations* (1964), pp. 643–664.

from the norms, we see that each view actually envelops a broad spectrum of attitudes. It seems clear that individual sensibilities find their expressions within the rich cultural heritage into which they happen to be born. The Western tradition's diversity of response to the problem of man-animal relationships is epitomized for White by Saint Francis of Assisi, whose perception of a unity of spirit in all creation resembled and in all likelihood stemmed ultimately from India.

This diversity of response can also be illustrated by the reactions of Europeans to their "discoveries" in the New World. The dominant Christian view in Saint Francis's day was not merely anthropocentric; it was rigidly ethnocentric too. Yet this ethnocentrism did not go unchallenged during the first centuries of European expansion. Renaissance exploration brought Christendom into contact not only with new fauna and flora, but with people whose racial and cultural characters seemed equally exotic. These beings walked about half naked, decorating their bodies with paint, plumage, stones, or shiny metal. They attached no special value to gold or silver, knew nothing of guns or books, spoke in unrecognizable tongues, and organized their lives within tribes. Where did these creatures belong in the scale of nature? They were not Christians, but they had human forms and they displayed human emotions. Were they rational people with human souls? That question was the nub of great theological and political controversies in Spain. Spanish economic interests required exploitation of the native populations of the Americas. But if these creatures had rational souls they should be treated as something above mere beasts. An Aristotelian scholar like Juan Ginés de Sepúlveda could justify Spanish conquests by insisting that the Indians of the New World fulfilled the philosopher's criteria for "natural slavery," a reduced, subhuman condition. But the prevailing tone of Spanish imperial ideology came to reflect the views of Bartolomeo de las Casas, the Dominican champion of the Indians, who preached the essential humanity of all peoples of the world, Christian and non-Christian alike.[8]

If the moral and political leaders of the time were uncertain as to the status of exotic peoples, what were less well-educated Western men to think? On the level of popular belief, as psychiatrist Henri F. Ellenberger tells us in our next article, Indians and other "savages" were regarded as curiosities in Europe and even were kept in zoos together with specimens of bizarre fauna. The breeds of the barely human included domestic products as well, so that the insane were now coming to be similarly displayed in "madhouses." This is only one of the parallels Ellenberger finds in his comparison of zoos and mental hospitals. Another is the simultaneous transformation of the zoo and asylum at the beginning of the nineteenth century.[9] Philippe Pinel, who unlocked the chains of inmates at the Salpêtrière, also helped convert the royal menagerie into the public zoological garden. Since Pinel's day, there have been metamorphoses in the avowed purposes of the two institutions. The zoo has become more open; there are attempts to replicate as closely as possible the animal's natural habitat. The mental hospital has become more closed; there are attempts to respect the patient as a human being with an illness. Professionals and laymen no longer view the inhabitants of either institution as curiosities, but as individuals (or species) with special, intrinsic needs. Despite their particular needs, residents of zoos and of mental hospitals have a number of similar problems. Ellenberger imaginatively describes the parallel psychological conditions of man and animal in the special state of captivity.

8. Lewis Hanke, *The Spanish Struggle for Justice in the Conquest of America* (Philadelphia, 1949); *Aristotle and the American Indians* (Chicago, 1959). J. H. Elliott, *The Old World and the New* (Cambridge, 1970), pp. 28–53.

9. Michel Foucault, *Madness and Civilization: A History of Madness in the Age of Reason* (New York, 1966); and David J. Rothman, *The Discovery of the Asylum* (Boston, 1971), discuss changing views of the mentally ill in Europe and America around 1800.

In the first flush of European expansion, perplexing captive savages stimulated theological debates and ethnological studies. But by the eighteenth century "uncivilized" people seemed to offer a newly self-conscious and introspective Western man glimpses of his own primordial condition. Buffon spoke for many when he wrote in 1749:

An absolute savage, such as the boy educated among the bears, . . . the young man in the forests of Hanover, or the little girl in the woods of France, would be a spectacle full of curiosity to a philosopher: in observing this savage he might be able precisely to ascertain the force of the appetites of nature; he might see the soul undisguised, and distinguish all its natural movements. And who knows whether he might not discover in it more mildness, more serenity and peace than in his own; whether he might not perceive, that virtue belongs more to the savage than to the civilized man, and that vice owes its birth to society.[10]

But the work of the physician Jean Itard with a "wild boy" captured in the Aveyron region of France marred the pretty picture of the noble savage. After failing in his efforts to teach the wild boy of Aveyron human speech, Itard was forced to this affirmation:

That man is inferior to a large number of animals in the pure state of nature, a state of nullity and barbarism that has been falsely painted in the most seductive colors; a state in which the individual, deprived of the characteristic faculties of his kind, drags on without intelligence or without feelings, a precarious life reduced to bare animal functions.[11]

In effect, Itard gave experimental substantiation to the Lockean environmentalism that dominated Enlightenment thought.

10. Georges-Louis Leclerc, comte de Buffon, *A Natural History, General and Particular,* 3d ed. (London, 1791), vol. 8, p. 39; as quoted by Greene, p. 182.
11. Jean-Marc-Gaspard Itard, *The Wild Boy of Aveyron,* trans. George and Muriel Humphrey (New York, 1962), pp. 49–50.

Even Rousseau, despite his popular reputation as glorifier of the noble savage, had stressed that man's ability to improve himself is what distinguishes him from animals. Man, unlike lower creatures, is not enslaved to instinct; he is free to alter his condition and even to remake his nature. Thus while man in the state of nature might closely resemble the apes, Rousseau held, he alone has potential for self-improvement.[12] To Enlightenment thinkers the Parisian child differs from the wild boy of Aveyron only because his potential is realized by his civilized environment. Civilization, the framework of myth, skill, and learning which is purposefully transmitted from one generation to the next, is the agent by which humans are transformed from helpless and solitary wild beasts into self-realizing social individuals.

In the fifth essay of this book, Joseph Wood Krutch argues that "civilization" can be extended to animals. Krutch, perhaps the greatest nature writer in the English language since Thoreau, began his career as an academic specializing in seventeenth- and eighteenth-century English literature, and much of his remarkable humanistic vision seems to have been shaped by a lifelong affinity for such writers as Samuel Johnson and Alexander Pope. In the essay reprinted here, Krutch takes as his starting axiom the idea that civilization develops human potentialities and then brilliantly observes that animals too have certain latent abilities which can be developed in a civilized environment. Pets, that is, animals who are tended and loved as individuals, grow to reveal a depth of personality that is never realized among members of the species living in the wild. In the end, Krutch goes beyond eighteenth-century formulations to argue that there is no fundamental difference between human and animal with regard to their abilities to realize under-

12. Jean Jacques Rousseau, *Discourse on the Origin of Inequality*, Part 1 (Paris, 1755).

developed potentialities in civilization.

If, as Lynn White maintains, the God of the Jewish and Christian traditions imposes an anthropocentric cast on the image of animals, Krutch's ethics would seem to be derived from a somewhat different system of values. Far from fixing a great gulf between animals and man and interpreting the role of the former as corollary of the purposes of the latter, Krutch finds kinship in the personality development of man and beast and implicitly advocates a respect for the individuality and private dignity of animals. Yet this dignity and individuality are depicted in distinctly *human* terms: the fulfillment of animal potential is as a pet in a man-constructed environment, and the nature of that fulfillment bears an extraordinary resemblance to the ideals of *homo sapiens*, Western individualistic variety. Krutch's application of the term "personality" to animals is highly appropriate, because in a sense his intention is to turn them into persons. This is less anthropocentric than it is anthropomorphic, the assignment to animals of human traits.

For anthropomorphism there is as long a tradition in the West as for anthropocentrism. The biblical passage recording the bestowal of lordship over animals to Noah and his descendants is followed immediately by God's promise never again to destroy the earth, a promise sealed by a convenant not only with man but with the totality of animal creation, "birds, cattle, and every wild beast as well—all that have come out of the ark, every living thing on earth." In the Hebraic vision, animals were regarded as capable of entering into a covenant with God. "When the bow is in the clouds, I will see it and remember the everlasting covenant between God and all living creatures, all flesh that is on the earth."[13] Similarly, animals could be held legally responsible for crimes, so that during biblical days and in medieval Europe it was common practice to bring animals

13. Gen. 9:8–17.

to trial and punish them upon conviction for such an infraction as attacking a human being or destroying property.[14] The assumption behind the covenant and the trials was that animals, quite as much as people, possess the qualities of free will and capacity for moral choice; hence they should be rewarded for virtuous actions and punished for criminal ones.

In the Renaissance, biblical anthropomorphism was overlaid with Greco-Roman animal imagery to produce the tradition of the "happy beast." Just as Buffon and others engaged in wistful nostalgia for the Golden Age of the "noble savage," another school of writers sought their social ideal not merely beyond civilization but beyond humanity. Pliny had found the condition of beasts enviable, for Mother Nature had endowed them with clothes upon arrival in this world. By contrast, Nature was a stepmother to man, for she brought him forth naked and helpless. To this biological advantage of animals Aelian and Plutarch had added the superiority of virtue: "They [animals] are more moral than we: they are not murderous, they respect their parents; they sacrifice themselves for their children. One might think Nature had given them to us as a lesson in good living."[15] Animals here are taken to represent human moral ideals. Centuries later, in the hands of Montaigne, this rather innocuous literary motif was transformed into an inflammatory doctrine. In his quasi-satirical essays the French skeptic attempted to show that animals are as noble, virtuous, and worthy of respect as man. Not only do animals exhibit gratitude,

14. For example, Exod. 21:28–29: "When an ox gores a man or a woman to death, the ox shall be stoned and its flesh shall not be eaten, but the owner of the ox is not to be punished. If, however, the ox has long been a gorer, and its owner, though warned, has failed to guard it, and it kills a man or a woman—the ox shall be stoned and its owner, too, shall be put to death." See also Edward P. Evans, *The Criminal Prosecution and Capital Punishment of Animals* (London, 1906).

15. George Boas, *The Happy Beast* (1933; reprinted New York, 1966), p. 19, paraphrasing Plutarch's arguments; see also *ibid.*, p. 15.

fidelity, magnanimity, and piety, but they are endowed with the supposedly uniquely human qualities, Reason and Science. Montaigne tried to demonstrate that animals can communicate among themselves and with us, remedy their own illnesses, learn to dance or to count, and teach their young. Predictably, Montaigne asserted that man's condition in civilization is worse than it was in animallike simplicity. In these ways, Montaigne put all animate creation on the same level. Nature provided all creatures with equal means of defense; humans are neither above nor below the others.[16] Now Montaigne's views evoked a storm of controversy. Traditional ecclesiastics objected that man had a unique place in creation, and moralists interpreted Montaigne's thesis as a license for men to behave like beasts. Yet Montaigne acquired many disciples, even some, including Charron, from among the Catholic clergy. Between the sixteenth and eighteenth centuries a great debate raged over the relative worth and virtue of animals.[17]

Now the terms "virtue" and "soul" have been deleted from the lexicon of modern biology, and anthropomorphism is universally shunned by the scientific community. Several of the authors of these readings carefully and explicitly deny their contamination by Montaignesque sentiments. Even so, don't we hear echoes of the seventeenth-century debate in present-day studies of aggression? For many writers, man alone is bent on vicious self-destruction; while for others, intraspecific aggression is a common feature in the animal kingdom.[18] The

16. *Ibid.*, pp. 3–10.

17. *Ibid.*, pp. 37–63, 118–155; Hester Hastings, *Man and Beast in French Thought of the Eighteenth Century* (Baltimore, 1936), pp. 64–174.

18. Among the writers who argue for the uniqueness of human aggression, see the scholarly work of Konrad Lorenz, *On Aggression* (New York, 1966); the popularization by Robert Ardrey, *The Territorial Imperative* (New York, 1966); and the psychoanalytical treatment by Gregory Rochlin, *Man's Aggression* (Boston, 1973). The spectrum of contemporary scientific views of the subject is summarized in Roger Johnson, *Aggression in Man and Animals* (Philadelphia, 1972).

former, more popular, position substantiates the twentieth-century mood of disillusionment with human society. Or has the mood perhaps colored scientific research? Today, just as in the age of Montaigne, the order and stability of animal society provide many people with an attractive contrast to the apparent chaos of human "civilization." When confidence in human nature ebbs, man may look to animals for a model and an alternative, but not for a reflection of himself.

While Krutch departs radically from his contemporaries by retaining confidence in man, the authors of our next essay admire the disdain by animals of human mores. According to novelists Frances and Richard Lockridge, people who anthropomorphize their pet house cats are doomed to misunderstand them. Great partisans of cats, the Lockridges' fondness appears based on the very failure of felines to conform to the human model. Cats, they write, stubbornly eschew man's ways and maintain a dignified independence of their masters. This the authors find attractive, especially in contrast to dogs, whom they characterize as essentially human beings *manqués*. Interestingly, the Lockridges play the role of careful behaviorists when they warn us against anthropomorphizing the cat, but this pose disappears when they turn to the "uncritical," "man-imitating" canine. Plainly, for these writers man's admiration for cats is analogous to his tolerance of people different from himself, while mastery over dogs is a displacement of his wish to enslave other men. Thus an egoistic anthropomorphism is at the heart of human-canine relationships, while man's dealings with felines reflect a more rationally detached "scientific" image in which human and animal meet on equal terms.

Ethological studies of undomesticated dogs help explain the apparent willingness of pet canines to follow a human master. Wild dogs are social animals who travel in packs and organize themselves in a hierarchy of dominance and submission. In this way dogs are biologically equipped to accept the principle of mastery; thus they fulfill an important precondition for domestication by man.[19] Cats, by contrast, are solitary animals in the wild; Kipling's legend notwithstanding, it is the genetic code that determines the feline style of association with man. This simple comparison of dogs and cats merely opens the imagination to the variety of situations that might produce "domesticated" animals. Our seventh reading, by F. E. Zeuner, follows a rigorously biological approach to this subject. Zeuner describes the relations of animal species to each other within the categories of parasitism, symbiosis, and so forth. Man as a cultural animal operates within these biological categories in his relationships with other species. Domestication is perhaps the most sophisticated level upon which species interact. But since it is based on the mutually complementary needs of man and beasts, domestication is a natural outgrowth of biologically simpler relationships. What is most fascinating, as Zeuner shows, is the variety of patterns of domestication. These match in diversity the conditions of human life throughout the world.

While some branches of modern biology seem detached from the debates of early modern Europe, others are firmly rooted in that epoch. We have already suggested that the current controversy over aggression in man and animals reflects the ancient question of the relative morality of humans and beasts. In the same way, the contemporary discussion of the applicability to man of behavioristic psychology revives a major issue in seventeenth-century science and philosophy. B. F. Skinner and other behaviorists attempt to apply to human behavior conclusions reached in laboratory experimentation with rats and other animals: they assume that despite the vast difference between species their fundamental psychological apparatus is essentially alike. The behaviorist thesis has not lacked challengers, for this

19. Michael W. Fox, *Understanding Your Dog* (New York, 1972), pp. 135–139, 155–167.

is an important subject to all students of man and nature. Noam
Chomsky, one of the most articulate critics of Skinner's methods and assumptions, has observed that in a sense this controversy reopens an issue dormant since the days of Descartes.[20]
According to the Cartesians, man's quality of "mind" makes
him palpably different from lower animals. Late in the seventeenth century, scientists abandoned this principle, as they
came to regard "mind" and "soul" as a priori categories impossible to investigate empirically. Since then the major thrust of
biological investigation has concentrated on the physiological
features which man shares with animals. Implicitly, biological
scientists have assumed that man's language and other cultural
abilities represent an extension of features present in lower
animals. But for the Cartesians, and in a sense for Chomsky,
these abilities are novel, unprecedented departures from other
forms of life. Modern behaviorists and seventeenth-century
anti-Cartesians find the key to man in studies of animal life,
while for Chomsky and the Cartesians the essence of man is his
very differentness from animals.

Ironically, behaviorists who reject the Cartesian view of
man's separateness from animals nevertheless share some of
Descartes's assumptions about nonhuman animals. Behaviorist
psychology attempts to explain animal (and human) behavior
within the rigorously mechanical limits of stimulus and response. Descartes, too, thought that animal (but not human)
behavior is governed by mechanical, measurable laws of movement. In Cartesian science, the only principle of movement for
animal bodies is the heat of the heart, which causes blood and
"animal spirits" to flow through the system. This operation is
completely involuntary and machinelike. In fact, Descartes
held that one could not distinguish a machine in the shape of

20. See especially Chomsky, *Cartesian Linguistics* (New York, 1966), pp.
1–31, 72–73.

an animal from the animal itself. In the Cartesian universe, man is set above animals by his conscious reason, as expressed in speech, the manifestation of the "rational soul." Animals have instincts that lead them to remarkably regular and perfect patterns of behavior. But since they lack the qualities of mind that can only be derived from a soul, they can experience no mental sensation, not even pain. This logical deduction was observed quite literally. In Cartesian anatomy classes dogs were dissected alive to demonstrate the functioning circulatory system. Their cries and howls were disregarded and dismissed as mere external motions. Live dissection became a popular pastime; a traveler on a long journey might break the monotony by observing the musculature and nervous system of a pinned frog.[21]

Cartesian science achieved its greatest impact in France, but even there many scientists and other men of letters were horrified by the theory and by its applications. It is said that the Cartesian philosopher, Malebranche, once kicked a pregnant dog that happened to roll near his feet. The dog whimpered, and Fontenelle, another eminent scientist who witnessed the scene, exclaimed his sympathy. But Malebranche responded, "What! Don't you know that it feels nothing?"[22] Outside France, the Cartesian beast-machine rarely took hold. In England, for example, poets, essayists, and journalists unanimously rejected the idea. Although Addison, Swift, and their contemporaries knew of the beast-machine, they chose to regard animals in more sympathetic ways. Animal superiority, as derived from Montaigne, was a popular theme, and many writers were attracted by the notion of the Cambridge Platonists that animals harbored a possibly immortal divine spark emanating from

21. The theories of René Descartes and their influence are described by Leonora Cohen Rosenfield, *From Beast-Machine to Man-Machine* (New York, 1940).
22. *Ibid.*, p. 70.

the World Spirit. The most widely accepted position, however, was the traditional idea that animals occupied an intermediate rung in the Great Chain of Being, lacking man's rational soul, but superior to lifeless matter in their capacity for feeling, perception, and memory.[23]

Quite apart from the intellectualized rationales, resistance to the Cartesian beast-machine in England and elsewhere emerged from a deep reservoir of emotional compassion for animals. Scattered references to kindness toward animals appear from the fifteenth century on, and during the Enlightenment this "humanitarian" attitude came to be considered an essential attribute of the civilized man.[24] By the early eighteenth century we find many outbursts entirely comparable to the animal protectionist rhetoric of more recent times. Bernard Mandeville's *The Fable of the Bees,* first published in 1714, contains this typically vivid statement:

When a large and gentle Bullock, after having resisted a ten times greater force of Blows than would have kill'd his Murderer, falls stunn'd at last, and his arm'd Head is fasten'd to the Ground with Cords; as soon as the wide Wound is made, and the Jugulars are cut asunder, what Mortal can without Compassion hear the painful Bellowings intercepted by his Blood, the bitter Sighs that speak the Sharpness of his Anguish, and the deep sounding Grones with loud Anxiety fetch'd from the bottom of his strong and palpitating Heart; Look on the trembling and violent Convulsions of his Limbs; see, while reeking Gore streams from him, his Eyes become dim and languid, and behold his Strugglings, Gasps and last Efforts for Life, the certain Signs of his approaching Fate? When a Creature has given such convincing and undeniable Proofs of the Terrors upon him, and the Pains and Agonies he feels, is there a Follower of *Descartes* so inur'd to Blood,

23. Wallace Shugg, "The Cartesian Beast-Machine in English Literature (1663–1750)," *Journal of the History of Ideas* 29 (1968): 279–280.
24. Hastings, pp. 175–278. On the subject of eighteenth-century humanitarianism in general, see Peter Gay, *The Enlightenment: An Interpretation*, 2 vols. (New York, 1967–69), 2:29–41, 396–447, and the references cited therein.

as not to refute, by his commiseration, the Philosophy of that vain Reasoner?[25]

The Cartesian beast-machine was surely Mandeville's primary target, but his graphic imagery also questions the tortures inflicted on animals for man's benefit. The suggestion of human involvement with all living things was explicitly articulated a generation later in Alexander Pope's *Essay on Man:*

> Has God, thou fool! work'd solely for thy good,
> Thy joy, thy pastime, thy attire, thy food?
> . . . .
> Is it for thee the lark ascends and sings?
> Joy tunes his voice, joy elevates his wings.
> Is it for thee the linnet pours his throat?
> Loves of his own and raptures swell the note.
> The bounding steed you pompously bestride,
> Shares with his lord the pleasures and the pride.
>
> . . . .
>   Know, Nature's children all divide her care;
> The fur that warms a monarch, warm'd a bear.
> While Man exclaims, "See all things for my use!"
> "See man for mine!" replies a pamper'd goose:
> And just as short of reason he must fall,
> Who thinks all made for one, not one for all.

Or, as the naturalist John Ray put it in his influential *The Wisdom of God Manifest in the Works of His creation* (1691): "If a good man be merciful to his beast then surely a good God takes pleasure that all his creatures enjoy themselves that have Life and sense and are capable of enjoying."[26]

Humanitarianism, then, as E. S. Turner observes in our final selection, was an idea before it was a movement. Turner pays close attention to the progress of this idea in eighteenth-century

25. Cited by Shugg, p. 288.
26. Quoted in Joseph Wood Krutch, *The World of Animals* (New York, 1961), p. 23.

England. He shows how the humanitarian sensibilities of a few literary men and women became a part of the gentlemanly moral code. Only after social attitudes—if not yet behavior—had been affected by the influence of upper- and middle-class literature, especially children's literature, did humanitarianism toward animals become a political issue and an institutionalized force in British life.

The humanitarian impulse of the modern West concerns itself with the treatment of both man and animals. A common system of morality inspired the RSPCA and the antislavery movement in nineteenth-century England, as contemporaries indicated when they dubbed an early defender of draught horses "the Wilberforce of hacks." This is just another example of the interplay between human relations and human relations with animals. In a sense, one can portray the current "ecology movement" as an extension of humanitarian concern from man and other living things to the totality of the earthly environment. The concern humanitarians have felt with their fellow men and their fellow animals is now being broadened to include plants, the land, waters, and atmosphere. If the values of his admittedly brief humanitarian tradition can allow Western man to include the nonaminal world in his deepened sense of empathy, perhaps we may yet find in our own culture the resources with which to fashion solutions to the environmental crisis, and so preserve mankind and the other animals.

1.

How Animals Live

H. Hediger

This brief outline of the question of where an animal lives, with reference to man's influence on it, is followed by the second equally simple question—how? Yet it is by no means as easy to answer as it might seem at first sight, for we know astonishingly little about the appropriate details of the animal's life.

It is important to consider the milieu—the surroundings in which it lives—not only in human psychology, where its importance is universally recognised, but in animal psychology as well. Domestic and laboratory animals do not live in their original milieu, but in a secondary man-made environment. Their behaviour is correspondingly distorted and unnatural.

We can see the need for insisting on this question of where and how an animal lives in the astonishing assertion—almost grotesque to a close observer of nature—made by a well-known student of human psychology, Pierre Janet (1935), when he said that the chief differentiation between animal and man is, that the former possesses no street system. Anyone who has observed animals, especially mammals, in freedom, knows how

SOURCE: From *The Psychology and Behaviour of Animals in Zoos and Circuses* by H. Hediger, Dover Publications, Inc., New York, 1955. Reprinted through the permission of the publisher.

untrue this statement is. In actual fact, countless animals had their own street systems long before man existed, and in many cases man has adopted animals' tracks, that is, he has shared them, and gradually re-shaped them into human paths and traffic routes. To take an extreme case for example; in North America many continental highways, and even railways, follow immemorial bison trails, as Martin Garretson has shown (1938, p. 54). In Africa to this day there are many rarely visited districts where animal tracks constitute the most convenient traffic routes for men—often the only practicable ones. I know from personal experience in Central Africa how pleasant it is, after stumbling painfully along through trackless bush, to strike all at once a hippo's track, running comfortably through the landscape like a well kept garden path.

But these streets, or animals' paths, of course are only lines of communication between single fixed points, the homes and colonies of the animals. Let us take a look, then, at the animal's home. It is surprising how much in common animal and human homes have, basically. In this similarity of subjective organization and of living space arrangements certainly lies one of the closest links between animals and man. In the animal's home, there are often special eating and drinking places, bathing and sleeping quarters, food stores and lavatory, sun-bathing terraces and nurseries, etc., etc. One locality only, the fireplace, found in even the most primitive man's hut, is absent in the case of every single animal.

One of the most decisive differences—perhaps indeed the most significant of all differences—between the animal's home and man's, lies in this fundamental distinction, seen from this particular viewpoint. The conquest of fire was literally the spark which originally kindled not only man's technique but his culture as well.

It may be worth while to summarize the latest research on the animal's home. A great deal of investigation was of course necessary in order to find out the natural living conditions of animals, and this work could not be carried out in the laboratory. Here the animal does not fit into the experimental arrangement, and the investigator has no choice but to follow up the animal, as quietly and as inconspicuously as possible. The prospects of answering the simple, but long-neglected questions about animals' living conditions are only possible if they are studied in undisturbed freedom, in their natural surroundings.

First and foremost, it is the field biologists who have done the best pioneer work here, in our own native woods and fields, as well as on the distant steppes, and in tropical rain forests. With the help of camera and binoculars, these men have chosen as subjects for exact observation individual animals, or else organized groups such as packs and herds, and have noted down in the minutest detail, with perseverance and devotion, the common daily life of a bird, a beast of prey, or a monkey.

With the objectivity of white-coated laboratory biologists taking readings from their precision instruments, field biologists on trek somewhere in the virgin forests of Indo-China, or the heart of Central America, have analysed the habits of gibbons, or the daily life of a group of howler monkeys.

For the outsider, perhaps one of the most surprising results of this field research is the fact—observed and confirmed countless times—that, with few exceptions, the so-called free-living animal does not wander about at will, but clings with remarkable tenacity to its little plot of earth, to its home, and usually leaves it only under the strongest compulsion. Such a home, that piece of land possessed by an individual, or shared by an organised group of individuals—a pack—is called in biological terms a territory. It is moreover vigorously defended against other members of the same species, especially of the same sex, and far less so against animals of different species.

Thus the fox, for instance, usually tolerates the presence of a badger in its neighbourhood, but would snap at another dog fox, and chase it away. The eagle even allows small song birds inside its eyrie, where they may sometimes nest, but another eagle would be remorselessly driven off by the owner. The swan, whose territory is about one third of a square mile, allows coots, little grebes, and gulls on its terrain, but not under any circumstances other male swans. The squirrel does not mind hares, wood mice, or stags in its woodland home but chases off in a rage all males of its own species that dare to set foot on its own territory.

In this way the territories of different species of animals may often overlap, or even coincide, though animals of the same species are forbidden the area. The territories of animals of the same species, for example foxes, blackbirds, or lions, would seem like the separate stones of a mosaic, if we could see them from the bird's eye view, each the same colour, and about the same size. Every mosaic of this sort has then superimposed on it several others, the territories of different species of animals, with stones of different colour and size. In the territory of a herd of chamois live marmots, jays, alpine jackdaws, and mountain salamanders as well. Different colours can overlap, but not stones of the same colour, as this would mean fighting, sometimes ruthless fatal combats.

Basically this is really rather like what happens among men. If a pigeon or a crow perches on the roof of our house, or a squirrel scampers round the garden, or a cat wanders in, we are usually indifferent. On the other hand, if we meet an uninvited member of our own species in the house or garden, our feelings of ownership are strongly aroused.

While small animals such as mice, lizards, or inch-long fish, have territories of up to ten square yards, lions or tigers need a dozen square miles or so. A couple of squirrels have a smaller territory than a couple of roe-deer, corresponding to their smaller food requirements, while a quail needs less than a hawk.

Carnivores always have larger territories than their herbivorous prey. For example, there must be room for many mouse territories in the territory of one fox, and for many antelope or zebra territories in that of a lion, since these herbivores must keep the carnivores self-supporting, so to speak, if the balance is to be maintained. Thus the size of an animal's territory is mainly dependent on two factors, the food requirements of its inhabitants and the products of its soil, either in the shape of animals to prey on, or food plants.

The size of a territory is not determined by the animal's desire to own a nice big park. It is even demonstrable that the territories are usually smaller in districts where food is abundant, than in those where food is scarce. Here one might mention in passing that in the zoo, where the animal is entirely relieved of the need to seek out its food, this being fully provided for it every day, the living space, the artificial territory in other words, can be very much smaller still.

In addition to the problem of the amount of space needed by an animal, the problem of its quality has long been neglected (Hediger, 1950, pp. 71 *et seq.*). Once again we are indebted to the field biologists for the essential information. To the animal that lives in it, a territory may not be of equal value from one end to the other, but is in fact in various ways subdivided into different localities, each associated with definite functions and significance. As we have pointed out, there are sleeping quarters, bathing places, food stores, etc.; in short, special inside arrangements differing for various species.

Knowledge of these conveniences, if I may use the term, is naturally of extreme importance in zoos, since one wants the inmates to feel as comfortable, as snug, and as much at home as possible. A small illustration may show what I mean. In Africa, I noticed that many termites' hills, standing up above the grass on the savannah, seemed to have their tops polished or worn away. It then transpired that elephants, buffaloes, and,

above all zebras, of the neighbourhood used to come regularly
and rub themselves luxuriously against these decorative termite castles. Often, round the bases of these cement-hard
humps built up to six feet or more by the insects, great tufts of
buffalo or zebra hair could be found. Thanks to their tracks, we
could see that zebras often came here from great distances, just
to rub and scratch themselves against the termites' nests. In
zebra territories, it is clear that such termitaries play an important part in grooming these handsome animals' striped coats.

On my return from Africa, I immediately had an artificial
termites' nest, made of a suitable cement mixture, fitted up in
the zebras' cage. When, for the first time, we opened the stable
doors, the zebras made straight for this termite castle, rubbing
so hard against it that they upset the whole contraption. This
was a clear enough indication that I was on the right track. A
new termites' nest was at once erected, reinforced this time,
and two attendants armed with whips had to keep off the zebras
until this piece of equipment, so vital for keeping their coats in
condition, had sufficiently hardened. It has been in daily use
ever since.

We do not need to go as far as Africa, however, to learn about
typical internal arrangements in animal territory, since these
can also be found among our native animals; deer, for example,
and rats. A most important feature in the deer's territory is the
wallow hole, or mud bath, which is hollowed out by the deer
themselves with their forefeet and, after generations of use,
may eventually widen out into a sort of pool. Wallowing in mud,
like most other activities, is not indulged in simply at the whim
of the individual concerned, but is an obligatory specific characteristic, similar for instance to providing stores, or defaecation
places, or laying down regular tracks, about which we shall have
something to say later.

There are wallowers and non-wallowers. The red deer belong
to the former, that is, to those animals in whose territory is

included a wallow hole; roe-deer on the other hand are not wallowing animals, and there is no wallow hole in their territories. We must differentiate clearly between wallowing and bathing, for this frequently takes place at quite a different part of the territory, though sometimes alongside it, as in the Indian rhinoceros.

Another most important locality in the deer's territory is the fighting ground, where, in the rutting season, rival stags fight it out. These special places are not just used for this special purpose for years, but for generations. It is quite untrue to assert that there are no traditions in the animal kingdom. There is very definitely an extremely strong tradition in space pattern, as is shown by the age-old salt licks, those places exceptionally rich in minerals that are constantly visited by animals to satisfy their salt hunger.

Many badgers' earths, and certain animal tracks trodden out over hard rock, are known to be centuries old (Neal, 1948). It is now part of the substance of our well-established knowledge of the lives of animals that most of them are confined within a regular network of localities, where for generations they have wallowed, bathed, fought, grazed, mated, slept, etc. Animals live in a fixed space-time system, i.e., in a pattern of fixed points, at which they perform definite functions at definite times (Hediger, 1950).

A particularly important type of locality in the animal's territory should not be overlooked, the so-called demarcation places, found with deer, and many other mammals. These exist usually on prominent twigs or branches, or tree stumps, or stones, to which the owner of the territory applies its own property marks, so to speak, in the form of a self-produced scent. We must remember that most mammals are macrosmatic, i.e., they have a literally superhuman sense of smell, by means of which they recognize faint traces of scent, which are quite beyond our powers of detection, as conspicuous signals.

Whilst human beings usually demarcate their buildings and homes optically by means of signboards and street numbers, macrosmatic animals naturally use scents. These are produced in parts of the body varying with the species concerned. In deer and among antelopes, the gland above the eye, the so-called antorbital gland, produces a strong-smelling, oily substance, a small quantity of which is rubbed off on to branches and the like. In this way the whole living space is virtually impregnated with the individual scent of the owner. Any other member of its own species is thus warned off by these scent signals, as soon as it enters an occupied territory.

In recent years many skin glands, whose function it is to provide scent for territory marking, have been discovered. We can clearly see in the zoo how extremely important these marking places are for macrosmatic animals. When animals of the same species are put together for the first time out of neighbouring enclosures, they do not as a rule look at each other to start with, but an examination of scent marks first takes place. While they are inspecting unfamiliar scent trails with their noses, the animals will often brush past each other. Only when the new area has become familiar olfactorily, does optical recognition of the inmates occur.

I will not go so far as to say that impregnation of space by scent—a kind of nest scent—plays a certain part with man as well, although much might perhaps be argued on this score. Monica Holzapfel-Meyer (1943, p. 28) is no doubt on the right lines in her summary of her own valuable research into animal psychology, as follows:

With regard to his division of space, man has remained very close to the animals. We probably imagine that to divide up our homes into bedrooms, dining rooms, drawing rooms, and kitchens is an achievement of civilisation, or culture. Even when there is only a single room, man will make similar divisions and will stick to them with the same tenacity as an animal. The urge to occupy definite fields of activity is so obvious that we only notice it when it ceases. This is sometimes the case in certain mental conditions, when the system of spacial constraints breaks down, giving way to a complete lack of discrimination between places of activity.

I had never properly realized the basic resemblance between man's way and animals' way of dividing up the earth's surface until on a flight over densely-populated Central Europe. The vivid chess-board pattern of arable and pasture was disconcertingly like the bird territories, as mapped out by Elliot Howard (1920), the pioneer of modern territory research thirty years ago.

And when over Central Africa, the plane flew high above isolated negro villages, the narrow tracks leading to the water holes, or the paths communicating between separate groups of stockaded huts, looked like nothing so much as animal tracks through the empty bush. Man is close to animals, not only as far as so-called fixed points, i.e., locations appointed for definite activities, are concerned, but also in his lines of communication, the tracks which link these together. We may watch a rat or a rhinoceros in the wild as it hugs its familiar tracks, and be struck in either case by the resemblance to a railway carriage running along its fixed rails.

Even in the huge bustling modern city, as G. Hinsche (1944) rightly points out, there are unmistakable counterparts of the animals' tracks. Anybody who today walks to business or to school will agree—on reflection—that he normally follows a definite route, always crossing the road at a certain spot, and preferring one particular side of the pavement, and so on, just as an animal in the zoo or in the wild favours certain little tracks, and gradually tramples them out into paths.

This remarkable reluctance to depart from the normal daily routine is strikingly illustrated in the zoo, during the morning rounds of inspection of the director and his assistants. This daily visitation, along the winding paths, past all the outer cages, through all the animals' houses, and the service rooms, takes up two to three hours. Naturally, it soon becomes automatic, so that one has practically to tear oneself away from the usual route to make a fresh variation. If, by way of exception, one does so, interesting facts in the field of human psychology emerge. Certain keepers may suddenly be encountered, no longer hard at work on cleaning operations, as was invariably the case of the routine tour, but perhaps having a quiet chat, or enjoying the illustrated magazines, or doing other equally astonishing things. As an animal psychologist, such things always remind one of the strength of attachment to habitual tracks!

Hinsche indulged in a scientifically useful bit of fun when he questioned more than 800 schoolchildren, aged ten to seventeen, about the details of their journey to school. As it turned out, most of them not only followed quite a definite path, for instance keeping to the right (or left) of a pillar box, walking under the projecting eaves of a roof, or over a man-hole cover, etc., but many indulged in little mannerisms at particular spots; for instance, touching a certain post, or stepping carefully over a crack in the asphalt, and so forth. If they failed to observe these rites of the road scrupulously, they thought that it would bring bad luck, e.g., low marks at school.

Only the familiar route made them feel safe and at ease; the animal, too, only feels safe in its traditional tracks. It has actually been experimentally shown that rats were able to reach safety much faster on their own network of tracks, when suddenly attacked by cats or dogs. On unfamiliar ground they were usually lost. Thus the primitive attachment of the animal to its own tracks is still clearly evident in man's behaviour. In fact it plays a considerable part, as Hinsche has shown, in our understanding of certain diseases of the human mind. From comparative observation, or even from a study of animal psychology in the zoo, we can, as scientific experience shows, gain some insight into a phenomenon so elementary yet socially significant, as sublime yet as primitive as nostalgia in man—that inspirer of the highest poetic creation as well as of criminal action. For it is a phenomenon that cannot be understood at all with reference to man alone. Here the viewpoint of comparative psychology taking into account animal behaviour, is indispensable.

In my book *Wild Animals in Captivity* (1950, pp. 31 *et seq.*), I drew attention to the importance of the quality of space compared with its quantity, usually all too often neglected. The most important part of the animal's territory, the focus, and in the truest sense the starting point, is the home, the nest, the place of maximum security. For human beings too, especially the children, this place is of the utmost importance.

There are two types of adults, as far as attitude to the home is concerned, the attached and the independent. The latter presumably include those who travel more often and—sometimes in the physiological sense—better than the stay-at-homes. Among individual races and nations there are obvious differences of this kind, for example, the Belgians, whose reputation as home-lovers may have some bearing on their colonial affairs.

Judging by his whole mental make-up, the human baby is just as dependent upon a home, in the biological sense, as an octopus or mouse, a fox or hippopotamus. In their psychotopes, a home is a basically important element, so much so that the lack of it may give rise to serious deficiency symptoms. In the literature of psychology, mental hygiene, and psychotherapeutics, there are exhaustive studies of the uprooted human being (waifs and strays). The reader is here referred to M. Pfister-Ammende's investigations (1950).

The secondary creation of a home is extemely important for those human beings, especially children, who have lost their natural homes, as happened on such a terrible scale in the Second World War, and have thus been the victims of uprooting with all its attendant evils. Those generous charitable organizations which took over the rescue work of children of this sort, noticed repeatedly an extremely significant fact. The well-meaning care given to these poor children in beautiful and spacious community rooms, turned out to be insufficient. All kinds of psychological deficiency symptoms kept on appearing, until the idea of dividing up the room, advocated among others by Professor S. Bayr-Klimpfinger, was adopted.

It consisted, in short, of splitting up the spacious day-rooms into separate territories, and in particular of making homes inside these compartments, within which the children could in a real sense feel at home. The Pestalozzi villages—conceived and first carried out by Walter Robert Corti in which, under optimum conditions, refugee children from all over the world can feel happy and settled in a home, in a familiar community, represent, both humanly and biologically, an excellent and ideal form of the successful artificial creation of a home. K. Heymann (1943) has vividly described how human children—like animals—often identify themselves with their house, i.e., with their home. There are of course animals that, in varying degrees, are actually physically connected with their houses, or whose bodies or bodily parts form offshoots of their homes. The rim of the limpet's conical house fits tightly over the spot chosen as its home on the rocks. The hermit crab's powerful claws act as a security precaution for the house which its body fits so perfectly. Many other animals have organs—often a specifically shaped head or tail—that act as a door. This phenomenon is known as phragmosis. The wart-hog (*Phacochoerus*) is the biggest example of this kind of thing. At night, it lives in underground tunnels of twelve to eighteen inches diameter. When alarmed, it dashes back to its home, swings quickly round at the entrance, and backs in, so that its powerful tusks project towards the entrance, forming a secure defence.

Too little attention has been paid to an important factor in the compulsory sharing of living quarters—both in the internment of human beings and in the captivity of animals—that is, to their psychotope, formerly called archetope. It has long been assumed that an animal is tied to, and even within—its living space, as far as its structure and activities are concerned; i.e., morphologically and physiologically (ecologically). In the mental field, a similar kind of adaptation to this biotope may be observed; a tuning in to the psychotope. When Russians from the spacious flat steppes were interned in a sub-alpine region in Switzerland, which we regard as a delightful holiday district, their reaction was marked, as M. Pfister described (1949). It transpired that these men from the boundless West Asian plains felt unhappy among our mountains. To them, these seemed sinister, oppressive. A similar eerie feeling of being oppressed, eventually becoming intolerable, is familiar to Europeans forced, as geologists, or colonial officials, to penetrate into the trackless primeval forest of Central Africa. After a few days, even thoroughly well-balanced men usually feel more or less depressed, and only regain their spirits when they see the light of day, or reach open paths. The opposite is true of the pygmies. For them, the open landscape is sinister and unbearable. Their psychotope is the thick virgin forest. Even those accustomed to continuous contact with white men move through the forest when going from place to place, if they can. Many animals clearly show strong psychic attachment to particular country, the psychotope. Here is a further instance of similarity between the spatial experience of men and of animals.

Another resemblance emerges, when one studies the distinguishing marks and boundaries of the living space, i.e., its territorial demarcation. While the individual, when defending its territory against the intrusion of outsiders, is directly concerned with acoustical, and especially with optical, marking, new possibilities arise with olfactory demarcation of territory. Scents, whether of dung, urine, or glandular secretion, are detachable from the body. They can literally be separated to act as place-reservations. The particle of dung, or the trace of secretion on the marking place, becomes, as Bilz shows, the *pars pro toto* (part for the whole), and continues to be efficacious even in the absence of its author.

Bilz, discussing the demarcation behaviour of bears and dogs (1940, p. 285), states:

Excrement and the image conveyed by it, frighten and even terrify the intruder. Is not this similar to magic? That tree-trunk scarred through being rubbed is still potent, even though the bear fell a victim to the hunter's gun weeks ago, and the scent banner unfurled against a tree stump by the dog continues to strike terror, even when the animal has long since changed masters and gone to live on another farm. Bear and dog alike have laid a ban on the district, to show that it is their home. Cave! Taboo!

It is likely that scent marks lose their effect after some weeks —that is why they are sometimes renewed by the animal once a day, or even oftener. Bilz's comparison of the scent-marking of territories with primitive man's magic and taboos seems to me significant. Among South Sea Islanders, and many other races living in a state of nature, practices occur that basically represent ownership tokens, such as marking freshly-cleared ground in the primeval forest, or the recognition marks applied to his kill when the hunter cannot take it with him at once. In many cases, it is not only a question of objective marking, but of laying a spell, or putting on a taboo—of defence measures against rivals and demons. Even as near to Europe as Morocco, I came across Berbers buying a tarry "secretion" from the medicine man in the bazaar, which they took home in short lengths of sheep's intestine, and applied to all four corners of a hut or house to ward off djinns, those abundant evil spirits. As with flight behaviour, so with demarcation behaviour in the human subjective world, the dangerous larger animals seem, in the course of development, to have been replaced by dangerous demons, and defence behaviour against animals gradually seems to have become superfluous, and have been correspondingly transferred to demons. Out of defences against rivals and enemies, magic was born.

REFERENCES

Bilz, R. (1940). *Pars pro toto. Ein Beitrag zur Pathologie menschlicher Affekte und Organfunktionen.* Leipzig.

Garretson, M. S. (1938). *The American Bison.* New York.

Hediger, H. (1950). *Wild Animals in Captivity. An Outline of the Biology of Zoological Gardens.* London.

Heymann, K. (1943). "Seelische Frühformen. Beiträge zur Psychologie der Kindheit." *Psychol. Praxis Basel,* I.

Hinsche, G. (1944). "Zur Genese der Stereotypien und Manieren. I. Wegeriten." *Psychiatr.-neurol. Wsche.,* XLVI.

Holzapfel-Meyer, M. (1943). "Affektive Grundlagen tierischen Verhaltens." *Schweiz. Zs. Psychol.,* II, 19–42.

Howard, E. (1920). *Territory in Bird Life.* London.

Janet, P. (1935). *Les débuts de l'intelligence.* Paris.

Neal, E. (1948). *The Badger.* London.

Pfister-Ammende, M. (1949). "Psychologische Erfahrungen mit sowjetrussischen Flüchtlingen in der Schweiz." *Die Psychohygiene,* II, ser. 2.

Pfister-Ammende, M. (1950). "Das Problem der Entwurzelung." *Schweiz. med. Wochenschrift,* 80, No. 6.

2.

Animals and Man
in Western Civilization

Lynn White, Jr.

A conversation with Aldous Huxley not infrequently put one at
the receiving end of an unforgettable monologue. About a year
before his lamented death he was discoursing on a favorite
topic: Man's unnatural treatment of nature and its sad results.
To illustrate his point he told how, during the previous summer,
he had returned to a little valley in England where he had spent
many happy months as a child. Once it had been composed of
delightful grassy glades; now it was becoming overgrown with
unsightly brush because the rabbits that formerly kept such
growth under control had largely succumbed to a disease, myx-
omatosis, that was deliberately introduced by the local farmers
to reduce the rabbits' destruction of crops. Being something of
a Philistine, I could be silent no longer, even in the interests of
great rhetoric. I interrupted to point out that the rabbit itself
had been brought as a domestic animal to England in 1176,

SOURCE: Lynn White, Jr., "The Historical Roots of Our Ecologic Crisis," *Science*,
    155 (March 10, 1967): 1203–1207. Copyright 1967 by the American Associ-
    ation for the Advancement of Science. Reprinted by permission of the
    author and *Science*.

presumably to improve the protein diet of the peasantry.

All forms of life modify their contexts. The most spectacular and benign instance is doubtless the coral polyp. By serving its own ends, it has created a vast undersea world favorable to thousands of other kinds of animals and plants. Ever since man became a numerous species he has affected his environment notably. The hypothesis that his fire-drive method of hunting created the world's great grasslands and helped to exterminate the monster mammals of the Pleistocene from much of the globe is plausible, if not proved. For six millennia at least, the banks of the lower Nile have been a human artifact rather than the swampy African jungle which nature, apart from man, would have made it. The Aswan Dam, flooding 5000 square miles, is only the latest stage in a long process. In many regions terracing or irrigation, overgrazing, the cutting of forests by Romans to build ships to fight Carthaginians or by Crusaders to solve the logistics problems of their expeditions, have profoundly changed some ecologies. Observation that the French landscape falls into two basic types, the open fields of the north and the *bocage* of the south and west, inspired Marc Bloch to undertake his classic study of medieval agricultural methods. Quite unintentionally, changes in human ways often affect nonhuman nature. It has been noted, for example, that the advent of the automobile eliminated huge flocks of sparrows that once fed on the horse manure littering every street.

The history of ecologic change is still so rudimentary that we know little about what really happened, or what the results were. The extinction of the European aurochs as late as 1627 would seem to have been a simple case of overenthusiastic hunting. On more intricate matters it often is impossible to find solid information. For a thousand years or more the Frisians and Hollanders have been pushing back the North Sea, and the process is culminating in our own time in the reclamation of the Zuider Zee. What, if any, species of animals, birds, fish, shore life, or plants have died out in the process? In their epic combat with Neptune have the Netherlanders overlooked ecological values in such a way that the quality of human life in the Netherlands has suffered? I cannot discover that the questions have ever been asked, much less answered.

People, then, have often been a dynamic element in their own environment, but in the present state of historical scholarship we usually do not know exactly when, where, or with what effects man-induced changes came. As we enter the last third of the twentieth century, however, concern for the problem of ecologic backlash is mounting feverishly. Natural science, conceived as the effort to understand the nature of things, had flourished in several eras and among several peoples. Similarly there had been an age-old accumulation of technological skills, sometimes growing rapidly, sometimes slowly. But it was not until about four generations ago that Western Europe and North America arranged a marriage between science and technology, a union of the theoretical and the empirical approaches to our natural environment. The emergence in widespread practice of the Baconian creed that scientific knowledge means technological power over nature can scarcely be dated before about 1850, save in the chemical industries, where it is anticipated in the eighteenth century. Its acceptance as a normal pattern of action may mark the greatest event in human history since the invention of agriculture, and perhaps in nonhuman terrestrial history as well.

Almost at once the new situation forced the crystallization of the novel concept of ecology; indeed, the word *ecology* first appeared in the English language in 1873. Today, less than a century later, the impact of our race upon the environment has so increased in force that it has changed in essence. When the first cannons were fired, in the early fourteenth century, they affected ecology by sending workers scrambling to the forests and mountains for more potash, sulfur, iron ore, and charcoal, with some resulting erosion and deforestation. Hydrogen bombs are of a different order: a war fought with them might alter the genetics of all life on this planet. By 1285 London had a smog problem arising from the burning of soft coal, but our present combustion of fossil fuels threatens to change the chemistry of the globe's atmosphere as a whole, with consequences which we are only beginning to guess. With the population explosion, the carcinoma of planless urbanism, the new geological deposits of sewage and garbage, surely no creature other than man has ever managed to foul its nest in such short order.

There are many calls to action, but specific proposals, however worthy as individual items, seem too partial, palliative, negative: ban the bomb, tear down the billboards, give the Hindus contraceptives and tell them to eat their sacred cows. The simplest solution to any suspect change is, of course, to stop it, or, better yet, to revert to a romanticized past: make those ugly gasoline stations look like Anne Hathaway's cottage or (in the Far West) like ghost-town saloons. The "wilderness-area" mentality invariably advocates deep-freezing an ecology, whether San Gimignano or the High Sierra, as it was before the first Kleenex was dropped. But neither atavism nor prettification will cope with the ecologic crisis of our time.

What shall we do? No one yet knows. Unless we think about fundamentals, our specific measures may produce new backlashes more serious than those they are designed to remedy.

As a beginning we should try to clarify our thinking by looking, in some historical depth, at the presuppositions that underlie modern techology and science. Science was traditionally aristocratic, speculative, intellectual in intent; technology was lower-classs, empirical, action-oriented. The quite sudden fusion of these two, towards the middle of the nineteenth century, is surely related to the slightly prior and contemporary democratic revolutions which, by reducing social barriers, tended to assert a functional unity of brain and hand. Our ecologic crisis is the product of an emerging, entirely novel, democratic culture. The issue is whether a democratized world can survive its own implications. Presumably we cannot unless we rethink our axioms.

THE WESTERN TRADITIONS OF TECHNOLOGY AND SCIENCE

One thing is so certain that it seems stupid to verbalize it: both modern technology and modern science are distinctively *occidental*. Our technology has absorbed elements from all over the world, notably from China; yet everywhere today, whether in Japan or in Nigeria, successful technology is Western. Our science is the heir to all the sciences of the past, especially perhaps to the work of the great Islamic scientists of the Middle Ages, who so often outdid the ancient Greeks in skill and perspicacity: al-Rāzī in medicine, for example, or ibn-al-Haytham in optics; or Omar Khāyyám in mathematics. Indeed, not a few works of such geniuses seem to have vanished in the original Arabic and to survive only in medieval Latin translations that helped to lay the foundations for later Western developments. Today, around the globe, all significant science is Western in style and method, whatever the pigmentation or language of the scientists.

A second pair of facts is less well recognized because they result from quite recent historical scholarship. The leadership of the West, both in technology and in science, is far older than the so-called scientific revolution of the seventeenth century or the so-called industrial revolution of the eighteenth century. These terms are in fact outmoded and obscure the true nature of what they try to describe—significant stages in two long and separate developments. By A.D. 1000 at the latest—and perhaps, feebly, as much as 200 years earlier—the West began to apply water power to industrial processes other than milling grain. This was followed in the late twelfth century by the harnessing of wind power. From simple beginnings, but with remarkable consistency of style, the West rapidly expanded its skills in the development of power machinery, laborsaving devices, and automation. Those who doubt should contemplate that most monumental achievement in the history of automation: the weight-driven mechanical clock, which appeared in two forms in the early fourteenth century. Not in craftsmanship but in basic technological capacity, the Latin West of the later Middle Ages far outstripped its elaborate, sophisticated, and esthetically magnificent sister cultures, Byzantium and Islam. In 1444 a great Greek ecclesiastic, Bessarion, who had gone to Italy, wrote a letter to a prince in Greece. He is amazed by the superiority of Western ships, arms, textiles, glass. But above all he is astonished by the spectacle of waterwheels sawing timbers and pumping the bellows of blast furnaces. Clearly, he had seen nothing of the sort in the Near East.

By the end of the fifteenth century the technological superiority of Europe was such that its small, mutually hostile nations could spill out over all the rest of the world, conquering, looting, and colonizing. The symbol of this technological superiority is the fact that Portugal, one of the weakest states of the Occident, was able to become, and to remain for a century, mistress of the East Indies. And we must remember that the technology of Vasco da Gama and Albuquerque was built by pure empiricism, drawing remarkably little support or inspiration from science.

In the present-day vernacular understanding, modern science is supposed to have begun in 1543, when both Copernicus and Vesalius published their great works. It is no derogation of their accomplishments, however, to point out that such structures as the *Fabrica* and the *De revolutionibus* do not appear overnight. The distinctive Western tradition of science, in fact, began in the late eleventh century with a massive move-

ment of translation of Arabic and Greek scientific works into
Latin. A few notable books—Theophrastus, for example—escaped the West's avid new appetite for science, but within less
than 200 years effectively the entire corpus of Greek and Muslim science was available in Latin, and was being eagerly read
and criticized in the new European universities. Out of criti-
cism arose new observation, speculation, and increasing distrust
of ancient authorities. By the late thirteenth century Europe
had seized global scientific leadership from the faltering hands
of Islam. It would be as absurd to deny the profound originality
of Newton, Galileo, or Copernicus as to deny that of the fourteenth century scholastic scientists like Buridan or Oresme on
whose work they built. Before the eleventh century, science
scarcely existed in the Latin West, even in Roman times. From
the eleventh century onward, the scientific sector of occidental
culture has increased in a steady crescendo.

Since both our technological and our scientific movements
got their start, acquired their character, and achieved world
dominance in the Middle Ages, it would seem that we cannot
understand their nature or their present impact upon ecology
without examining fundamental medieval assumptions and developments.

MEDIEVAL VIEW OF MAN AND NATURE

Until recently, agriculture has been the chief occupation
even in "advanced" societies; hence, any change in methods of
tillage has much importance. Early plows, drawn by two oxen,
did not normally turn the sod but merely scratched it. Thus,
cross-plowing was needed and fields tended to be squarish. In
the fairly light soils and semi-arid climates of the Near East and
Mediterranean, this worked well. But such a plow was inappro-
priate to the wet climate and often sticky soils of northern

Europe. By the latter part of the seventh century after Christ, however, following obscure beginnings, certain northern peasants were using an entirely new kind of plow, equipped with a vertical knife to cut the line of the furrow, a horizontal share to slice under the sod, and a moldboard to turn it over. The friction of this plow with the soil was so great that it normally required not two but eight oxen. It attacked the land with such violence that cross-plowing was not needed, and fields tended to be shaped in long strips.

In the days of the scratch-plow, fields were distributed generally in units capable of supporting a single family. Subsistence farming was the presupposition. But no peasant owned eight oxen: to use the new and more efficient plow, peasants pooled their oxen to form large plow-teams, originally receiving (it would appear) plowed strips in proportion to their contribution. Thus, distribution of land was based no longer on the needs of a family but, rather, on the capacity of a power machine to till the earth. Man's relation to the soil was profoundly changed. Formerly man had been part of nature; now he was the exploiter of nature. Nowhere else in the world did farmers develop any analogous agricultural implement. Is it coincidence that modern technology, with its ruthlessness toward nature, has so largely been produced by descendants of these peasants of northern Europe?

This same exploitive attitude appears slightly before A.D. 830 in Western illustrated calendars. In older calendars the months were shown as passive personifications. The new Frankish calendars, which set the style for the Middle Ages, are very different: they show men coercing the world around them—plowing, harvesting, chopping trees, butchering pigs. Man and nature are two things, and man is master. . . .

The victory of Christianity over paganism was the greatest psychic revolution in the history of our culture. It has become fashionable today to say that, for better or worse, we live in "the post-Christian age." Certainly the forms of our thinking and language have largely ceased to be Christian, but to my eye the substance often remains amazingly akin to that of the past. Our daily habits of action, for example, are dominated by an implicit faith in perpetual progress which was unknown either to Greco-Roman antiquity or to the Orient. It is rooted in, and is indefensible apart from, Judeo-Christian teleology. The fact that Communists share it merely helps to show what can be demonstrated on many other grounds: that Marxism, like Islam, is a Judeo-Christian heresy. We continue today to live, as we have lived for about 1700 years, very largely in a context of Christian axioms.

What did Christianity tell people about their relations with the environment?

While many of the world's mythologies provide stories of creation, Greco-Roman mythology was singularly incoherent in this respect. Like Aristotle, the intellectuals of the ancient West denied that the visible world had had a beginning. Indeed, the idea of a beginning was impossible in the framework of their cyclical notion of time. In sharp contrast, Christianity inherited from Judaism not only a concept of time as nonrepetitive and linear but also a striking story of creation. By gradual stages a loving and all-powerful God had created light and darkness, the heavenly bodies, the earth and all its plants, animals, birds, and fishes. Finally, God had created Adam and, as an afterthought, Eve, to keep man from being lonely. Man named all the animals, thus establishing his dominance over them. God planned all of this explicitly for man's benefit and rule: no item in the physical creation had any purpose save to serve man's purposes. And, although man's body is made of clay, he is not simply part of nature: he is made in God's image.

Especially in its Western form, Christianity is the most anthropocentric religion the world has seen. As early as the second century both Tertullian and Saint Irenaeus of Lyons were insisting that when God shaped Adam he was foreshadowing the image of the Incarnate Christ, the Second Adam. Man shares, in great measure, God's transcendence of nature. Christianity, in absolute contrast to ancient paganism and Asia's religions (except, perhaps, Zoroastrianism), not only established a dualism of man and nature but also insisted that it is God's will that man exploit nature for his proper ends.

At the level of the common people this worked out in an interesting way. In antiquity every tree, every spring, every stream, every hill had its own *genius loci,* its guardian spirit. These spirits were accessible to men, but were very unlike men; centaurs, fauns, and mermaids show their ambivalence. Before one cut a tree, mined a mountain, or dammed a brook, it was important to placate the spirit in charge of that particular situation, and to keep it placated. By destroying pagan animism, Christianity made it possible to exploit nature in a mood of indifference to the feelings of natural objects.

It is often said that for animism the Church substituted the cult of saints. True; but the cult of saints is functionally quite different from animism. The saint is not *in* natural objects; he may have special shrines, but his citizenship is in heaven. Moreover, a saint is entirely a man; he can be approached in human terms. In addition to saints, Christianity of course also had angels and demons inherited from Judaism and perhaps, at one remove, from Zoroastrianism. But these were all as mobile as the saints themselves. The spirits *in* natural objects, which formerly had protected nature from man, evaporated. Man's effective monopoly on spirit in this world was confirmed, and the old inhibitions to the exploitation of nature crumbled.

When one speaks in such sweeping terms, a note of caution is in order. Christianity is a complex faith, and its consequences differ in differing contexts. What I have said may well apply to the medieval West, where in fact technology made spectacular advances. But the Greek East, a highly civilized realm of equal

Christian devotion, seems to have produced no marked technological innovation after the late seventh century, when Greek
fire was invented. The key to the contrast may perhaps be
found in a difference in the tonality of piety and thought which
students of comparative theology find between the Greek and
the Latin churches. The Greeks believed that sin was intellectual blindness, and that salvation was found in illumination,
orthodoxy—that is, clear thinking. The Latins, on the other
hand, felt that sin was moral evil, and that salvation was to be
found in right conduct. Eastern theology has been intellectual-
ist. Western theology has been voluntarist. The Greek saint
contemplates; the Western saint acts. The implications of Christianity for the conquest of nature would emerge more easily in
the Western atmosphere.

The Christian dogma of creation, which is found in the first
clause of all the Creeds, has another meaning for our comprehension of today's ecologic crisis. By revelation, God had given
man the Bible, the Book of Scripture. But since God had made
nature, nature also must reveal the divine mentality. The religious study of nature for the better understanding of God was
known as natural theology. In the early Church, and always in
the Greek East, nature was conceived primarily as a symbolic
system through which God speaks to men: the ant is a sermon
to sluggards; rising flames are the symbol of the soul's aspiration.
This view of nature was essentially artistic rather than scientific.
While Byzantium preserved and copied great numbers of ancient Greek scientific texts, science as we conceive it could
scarcely flourish in such an ambience.

However, in the Latin West by the early thirteenth century
natural theology was following a very different bent. It was
ceasing to be the decoding of the physical symbols of God's
communication with man and was becoming the effort to understand God's mind by discovering how his creation operates.
The rainbow was no longer simply a symbol of hope first sent

to Noah after the Deluge: Robert Grosseteste, Friar Roger Bacon, and Theodoric of Freiberg produced startlingly sophisticated work on the optics of the rainbow, but they did it as a venture in religious understanding. From the thirteenth century onward, up to and including Leibnitz and Newton, every major scientist, in effect, explained his motivations in religious terms. Indeed, if Galileo had not been so expert an amateur theologian he would have got into far less trouble: the professionals resented his intrusion. And Newton seems to have regarded himself more as a theologian than as a scientist. It was not until the late eighteenth century that the hypothesis of God became unnecessary to many scientists.

It is often hard for the historian to judge, when men explain why they are doing what they want to do, whether they are offering real reasons or merely culturally acceptable reasons. The consistency with which scientists during the long formative centuries of Western science said that the task and the reward of the scientist was "to think God's thoughts after him" leads one to believe that this was their real motivation. If so, then modern Western science was cast in a matrix of Christian theology. The dynamism of religious devotion, shaped by the Judeo-Christian dogma of creation, gave it impetus.

AN ALTERNATIVE CHRISTIAN VIEW

We would seem to be headed toward conclusions unpalatable to many Christians. Since both *science* and *technology* are blessed words in our contemporary vocabulary, some may be happy at the notions, first, that, viewed historically, modern science is an extrapolation of natural theology and, second, that modern technology is at least partly to be explained as an occidental, voluntarist realization of the Christian dogma of man's transcendence of, and rightful mastery over, nature. But, as we now recognize, somewhat over a century ago science and technology—hitherto quite separate activities—joined to give mankind powers which, to judge by many of the ecologic effects, are out of control. If so, Christianity bears a huge burden of guilt.

I personally doubt that disastrous ecologic backlash can be avoided simply by applying to our problems more science and more technology. Our science and technology have grown out of Christian attitudes toward man's relation to nature which are almost universally held not only by Christians and neo-Christians but also by those who fondly regard themselves as post-Christians. Despite Copernicus, all the cosmos rotates around our little globe. Despite Darwin, we are *not*, in our hearts, part of the natural process. We are superior to nature, contemptuous of it, willing to use it for our slightest whim. The newly elected governor of California, like myself a churchman, but less troubled than I, spoke for the Christian tradition when he said (as is alleged), "when you've seen one redwood tree, you've seen them all." To a Christian a tree can be no more than a physical fact. The whole concept of the sacred grove is alien to Christianity and to the ethos of the West. For nearly two millennia Christian missionaries have been chopping down sacred groves, which are idolatrous because they assume spirit in nature.

What we do about ecology depends on our ideas of the man-nature relationship. More science and more technology are not going to get us out of the present ecologic crisis until we find a new religion, or rethink our old one. The beatniks, who are the basic revolutionaries of our time, show a sound instinct in their affinity for Zen Buddhism, which conceives of the man-nature relationship as very nearly the mirror image of the Christian view. Zen, however, is as deeply conditioned by Asian history as Christianity is by the experience of the West, and I am dubious of its viability among us.

Possibly we should ponder the greatest radical in Christian history since Christ: Saint Francis of Assisi. The prime miracle

of Saint Francis is the fact that he did not end at the stake, as
many of his left-wing followers did. He was so clearly heretical
that a general of the Franciscan Order, Saint Bonaventura, a
great and perceptive Christian, tried to suppress the early accounts of Franciscanism. The key to an understanding of Francis is his belief in the virtue of humility—not merely for the
individual but for man as a species. Francis tried to depose man
from his monarchy over creation and set up a democracy of all
God's creatures. With him the ant is no longer simply a homily
for the lazy, flames a sign of the thrust of the soul toward union
with God; now they are Brother Ant and Sister Fire, praising
the Creator in their own ways as Brother Man does in his.

Later commentators have said that Francis preached to the
birds as a rebuke to men who would not listen. The records do
not read so: he urged the little birds to praise God, and in
spiritual ecstasy they flapped their wings and chirped rejoicing.
Legends of saints, especially the Irish saints, had long told of
their dealings with animals but always, I believe, to show their
human dominance over creatures. With Francis it is different.
The land around Gubbio in the Apennines was being ravaged
by a fierce wolf. Saint Francis, says the legend, talked to the wolf
and persuaded him of the error of his ways. The wolf repented,
died in the odor of sanctity, and was buried in consecrated
ground.

What Sir Steven Ruciman calls "the Franciscan doctrine of
the animal soul" was quickly stamped out. Quite possibly it was
in part inspired, consciously or unconsciously, by the belief in
reincarnation held by the Cathar heretics who at that time
teemed in Italy and southern France, and who presumably had
got it originally from India. It is significant that at just the same
moment, about 1200, traces of metempsychosis are found also
in western Judaism, in the Provençal *Cabbala*. But Francis held
neither to transmigration of souls nor to pantheism. His view of
nature and of man rested on a unique sort of pan-psychism of

all things animate and inanimate, designed for the glorification of their transcendent Creator, who, in the ultimate gesture of cosmic humility, assumed flesh, lay helpless in a manger, and hung dying on a scaffold.

I am not suggesting that many contemporary Americans who are concerned about our ecologic crisis will be either able or willing to counsel with wolves or exhort birds. However, the present increasing disruption of the global environment is the product of a dynamic technology and science which were originating in the Western medieval world against which Saint Francis was rebelling in so original a way. Their growth cannot be understood historically apart from distinctive attitudes toward nature which are deeply grounded in Christian dogma. The fact that most people do not think of these attitudes as Christian is irrelevant. No new set of basic values has been accepted in our society to displace those of Christianity. Hence we shall continue to have a worsening ecologic crisis until we reject the Christian axiom that nature has no reason for existence save to serve man.

The greatest spiritual revolutionary in Western history, Saint Francis, proposed what he thought was an alternative Christian view of nature and man's relation to it: he tried to substitute the idea of the equality of all creatures, including man, for the idea of man's limitless rule of creation. He failed. Both our present science and our present technology are so tinctured with orthodox Christian arrogance toward nature that no solution for our ecologic crisis can be expected from them alone. Since the roots of our trouble are so largely religious, the remedy must also be essentially religious, whether we call it that or not. We must rethink and refeel our nature and destiny. The profoundly religious, but heretical, sense of the primitive Franciscans for the spiritual autonomy of all parts of nature may point a direction. I propose Francis as a patron saint for ecologists.

3.

The Unity of Life
in Indian Religion

W. Norman Brown

If we were to ask a devout Christian and a devout Hindu who
one's brother is, we would expect very different answers. The
Christian view is that one's brother is his fellow man, or, as it
is put in both the Old and New Testament, his neighbor is his
fellow man, whom he should love as himself (Lev. 19.18; Matt.
19.19 and 22.39; Mark 12.33). To illustrate this view the Christian might cite the parable of the good Samaritan (Luke 10.
29–37, which has a moral that was apparently questionable to
Jesus' audience as being extreme, too latitudinarian. But to the
Hindu the Christian definition would appear narrow, restric-
tive, and therefore indefensible and untenable. The Hindu considers that one's brother or neighbor is not merely humankind
but the lower animals as well. He recognizes that all life is a
unity. This view is now, and for two millennia or more has been,
a feature of Hinduism, Jainism, and Buddhism, the three great

SOURCE: W. Norman Brown, *Man in the Universe: Some Continuities in Indian
Thought* (Berkeley and Los Angeles, 1966), pp. 43–49, 65–67. Originally
published by the University of California Press; reprinted by permission of
the Regents of the University of California.

religions that are native to India. As a common Indian value, held to be valid in both traditional and modern India, it has had important intellectual and ethical consequences and ramifications, and prompts interesting questions. It is the purpose of this lecture to examine some of the history of the idea, observe some of its consequences and ramifications, and consider some of the questions it raises.

The most important consequence is the ethical precept that one should not inflict injury upon any living creature. It is a matter of simple logic that belief in the unity of life should lead to the doctrine that wherever life exists, it should be inviolable. The Indian term for the doctrine is Ahinsa *(ahiṃsā)*, which is variously translated as "harmlessness, noninjury, nonviolence," the last being Gandhi's rendering. The word *ahiṃsā* is Sanskrit and is a negative formation, made by prefixing the negative element *a-* to the noun *hiṃsā* which means "injury." Hence *ahiṃsā* means non-*hiṃsā*, the opposite of *hiṃsā* or "injury." But though the term Ahinsa is negative in formation, the idea it expresses is positive, for it includes the practise of "friendliness" *(maitrī)* and "compassion" *(karuṇā)*. Ahinsa is the most important and most widely preached of all Indian ethical teachings, and the three faiths unite in supporting the frequently quoted Sanskrit aphorism *ahiṃsā paramo dharmaḥ*, "Ahinsa is the highest religion," which is often reinforced by the statement that however much religions may differ on other points, they agree on this. Gandhi expressed that view in different phraseology when he said, "I am fascinated by the law of love. It is the philosopher's stone for me. I know that Ahinsa alone can provide a remedy for our ills."

Many kinds of persuasion are used in the traditional literature of Buddhism, Jainism, and Hinduism to support the teaching of Ahinsa. Often the method is direct exhortation in sermons; often—and perhaps more effectively—it is by the use of exempla to illustrate the rewards of practicing Ahinsa or the retribution for violating it. A kind act to an animal, especially an act that involves self-denial or pain for the doer, may be shown to bring one a happier lot in a future existence. On the other hand, injury of an animal may lead to condign punishment. A Buddhist story (Jātaka 18) which includes a sectarian sideswipe at Brahmanical Hinduism, illustrates this.

A Brahman was preparing to make an offering to his dead ancestors by sacrificing a goat, and had turned the animal over to his disciples for the preliminary bathing and garlanding. While this was going on, the goat suddenly acquired recollection of its previous existences and thereupon burst into a loud peal of laughter, like the breaking of a pot. But a moment later it fell into a fit of weeping. The disciples reported this unprecedented behavior to the Brahman, who asked the goat, "Why did you laugh?" "Because," replied the goat, "long ago in a previous existence I was a Brahman like you and I too celebrated just such a sacrifice to the dead. As a result I was doomed to be reborn as a goat for 500 successive existences, and in each existence to have my head cut off. I have already suffered this fate 499 times, and now when my head is cut off for the 500th time, my punishment will come to an end. Therefore in my joy I laughed." "And why," asked the Brahman, "did you weep?" "I wept," said the goat, "when I thought of the 500 existences of sorrow which you are about to bring upon yourself by cutting off my head." "Never fear," said the Brahman, "I shall not sacrifice you and you shall escape the pain of having your head cut off." "It will make no difference for you to spare me," said the goat, "my head must inevitably be cut off." The Brahman, however, gave orders to his disciples to see that no harm came to the goat. Once free, the goat ran over to a ledge of rock and stretched its head out to nibble the leaves on a bush growing there. At that moment out of the clear sky came a sudden bolt of lightning, which split off a sliver from the overhanging rock, and this sliced off the goat's outstretched head as clean as with an executioner's knife.

Besides supporting Ahinsa with threats of disastrous consequences, the religious literature has many legends to illustrate the theme that the genuinely good and wise practice Ahinsa as a positive virtue. One such legend among the Jains is that of Nemi, the twenty-second of the twenty-four world Saviors who that faith says have appeared successively in the past billions of years to teach mankind the eternal truth and the way to gain release from the otherwise beginningless and endless round of rebirths.

Nemi is said in the legend to have been born a prince, as were all the Jain Saviors, and was raised in comfort and splendor. He is represented as a contemporary and cousin of the Hindu hero and teacher Krishna, who is an incarnation *(avatāra)* of the god Vishnu and the reciter of the Bhagavad Gītā. After Nemi as a wonder child and gifted youth had performed a number of marvelous feats, his father wanted him to marry, but Nemi, already obsessed with following the call of religion, demurred. The king then asked Krishna to use his influence on him, and Krishna turned the assignment over to his wives. They joked Nemi at having reached marriageable age but remaining unwed. He answered that there was no profit in associating with women and getting married; he preferred to seek perfection and release from rebirth. Then Krishna himself spoke to Nemi, reminding him that all previous world Saviors had married and raised families before abandoning worldly affairs to follow the quest of religion. He should therefore marry and please his father. Nemi reluctantly consented, and a beauteous bride was selected for him, the daughter of a neighboring king and Nemi's wife in previous existences. On the appointed day, the bride, bathed and adorned, and filled with agitation and delight at securing so rare a bridegroom, was seated in a splendidly decorated marriage pavilion waiting for Nemi. He, too, fully ornamented, was on his way, riding in a noble chariot. But suddenly he heard a confused hullabaloo of piteous cries. He looked around and saw that the cries came from a pen filled with fowl, deer, and other animals waiting to be slaughtered for the wedding feast. The thought of their imminent death revolted him, and filled with disgust at the worldly life and now solidly confirmed in his intent to seek the goal of religion, he stripped off his jewels and finery to give it all to his charioteer and ordered him to turn the chariot around and head for the open spaces. Thus he abandoned his unclaimed bride so that he could become a houseless mendicant wanderer searching for salvation. In the sequel the bride also became an ascetic successfully seeking release from the misery of rebirth. The story of Nemi is one of the best-loved in all Jain hagiography, and it is copiously told in literary texts, illustrated in miniature paintings, and carved in wood and stone in temples. It moves the compassionate heart of Jainism and emphasizes for Jains the brotherhood of man with the subhuman creation.

Belief in the inviolability of all life naturally leads to the practice of vegetarianism. Meat-eating is abhorred today by strict Jains and Hindus and many Buddhists much as cannibalism is by us. The prohibition extends even to the eating of eggs or any dishes made with eggs. In our time the practice of vegetarianism as an accompaniment to the practice of Ahinsa was an ethical essential in Gandhi's program. He demanded a vow of Ahinsa and vegetarianism from all those who came to live in his hermitage *(āshram)* and continually preached the doctrine in his speeches and writing.

For Hindus today and for a good many centuries in the past, perhaps for as much as two millennia, the doctrine of Ahinsa has reached its apex with respect to the cow. That animal has for them a special sanctity, entitling it not only to protection and inviolability but to actual worship as well. Since the arrival of the Muslims in India, first in the eighth century, the cow has continuously been one of the chief causes of quarrels and bloody riots between Hindus and Muslims, for the latter, like Christians, have no feeling that the cow is sacred and instead slaughter it and eat its flesh. To Gandhi the cow was "a poem of pity," and cow-protection was a fundamental item in his program for the regeneration of India. He always wanted it to be a goal of nationalism. His insistence upon the point, like that of the great nationalist leader Tilak before him, was never considered reasonable or even intelligible or tolerable by Muslims and was an important factor in the failure of the Indian National Congress to get full Muslim cooperation in the struggle against the British. After the attainment of Independence, when a new constitution was adopted in 1950, one of the directive principles of state policy prescribed that the government is to prevent "slaughter of cows and calves, and other milch and draught cattle"—a provision that may or may not have been included partly for economic reasons but certainly was a concession to Hindu religious sensibilities. A number of Indian states today have cow-protection provisions; some prohibit the slaughter of old and decrepit cattle and support at public expense refuges or sanctuaries (gosadan) for them. There are a number of voluntary associations propagandizing for prohibition of cow slaughter in those states where it is permitted.

Questions naturally come to one's mind concerning the origin of the various ideas that all life, human and animal, is a unity; that all life, again both human and animal, is inviolable; and that for Hindus the cow is especially inviolable, that it is in fact sacred and to be worshipped. Let me start in considering these questions by surveying the data which Indian literature offers us concerning the unity of human and animal life. A basis for this belief appears first in connection with the doctrine of rebirth, also variously known as transmigration, metempsychosis, the round of existence. . . .

In the Upanishads, as we have seen, the doctrine of Ahinsa is a late arrival and has an undefined content. That is also true in the Bhagavad Gītā. It seems clear that the idea would not have existed in those texts but for the belief in the doctrine of rebirth,

when that belief came to include rebirth on earth in animal
form as well as human form depending upon one's actions. But
once the latter idea was accepted, namely, that transmigration
carries an individual into all kinds of bodies, then it followed
that human beings and animals were considered related, that
basically they were identical, and that every living person has
been an animal many times in the past and all but those rarest
ones who succeed in escaping from the round of existence will
be animals an indefinite number of times in the future. Hence
human life and animal life are one, and it is apparent that we
should treat animals with the same consideration that we show
human beings. In so doing we satisfy our own ethical egoism.

All this sounds plausible enough, but I fear it is all only a chain
of rationalization. The ideas of Ahinsa and the unity of all life
did not have their origin in Vedic Aryan thought, but entered
it from outside. The environment in which those ideas were at
home was that of Jainism and Buddhism. In them Ahinsa was
a dominant and original, not supplemental, feature. It was the
first of the vows which every monk must take on entering the
order of the two faiths, and its importance was developed in
countless sermons in the earliest as well as the later strata of
their literature. Jainism and Buddhism were wholeheartedly
preaching Ahinsa at a time when it was only inconspicuously
being accepted in the Upanishads and the Bhagavad Gītā. It is
a good guess, having a high amount of probability, that the
precept of Ahinsa and the doctrine of the unity of all life had
their origin in non-Aryan culture, with which Aryan culture was
blending at that time in northern India. Even if this be true, we
still cannot see the origins of the ideas. I believe them to lie
deep in prehistoric folk belief and agree with Professor Ludwig
Alsdorf that Ahinsa is at bottom a magic-ritualistic tabu on taking life,[1] though, of course, there are no documents of the first

1. Ludwig Alsdorf, "Beiträge zur Geschichte von Vegetarismus und Rinder-

half of the first millennium to prove this. So, too, we may not unreasonably regard the conception of the unity of life as being at base a generalized primitive folkloristic totemism, though again we cannot support such a view with substantiating documentation from the first millennium B.C. This pair of assumptions would provide an acceptable basis for the prevalence in India of the widespread belief in the unity of life as a religious axiom and the derivation from it of the doctrine of Ahinsa as the country's prime ethical value. Neither of the ideas is rational in the sense of being based upon processes of reasoning; rather they are congenital, inherent, visceral, emotional in their sources but at the same time all the stronger and more deeply rooted for being so, and the more likely, therefore, to extend their already long existence.

---

verehrung in Indien," *Abhandlungen der Geistes- und Sozialwissenschaftlichen Klassen*, No. 6 (1961), Akademie der Wissenschaften und der Literatur in Mainz, pp. 571, 589, 610: "sie [*Ahiṃsā*] hat ursprünglich mit Ethik in unserem Sinne nichts zu tun sondern ist ein magisch-ritualistiches Tabu auf das Leben, das in keiner seiner Formen zerstört werden darf" (p. 517). ("It [*ahiṃsā*] originally had nothing to do with ethics as we understand the term, but instead is a magical-ritualistic taboo against destroying life in any of its forms." Editors' translation.)

4.

The Mental Hospital
and the Zoological Garden

Henri F. Ellenberger

"If there were no animals," declared Buffon, "human nature
would be far more incomprehensible."[1] The great naturalist
meant only the physiological nature of man, since he could not
suspect how much we might learn about the human psyche
from studying animals. Today we know that animal psychology,
insofar as it uncovers basic psychological processes common to
man and animal, may enlighten us about certain obscure sides
of the human spirit.

To be sure, such studies are riddled with difficulties. Two
opposing pitfalls are to be avoided. One, the anthropomorphic
fallacy, projects upon animals our ways of seeing humans. This
fallacy is that of the man who regards the caged lion as a noble
warrior dreaming nostalgically of his native forest while he

SOURCE: H. F. Ellenberger, "Jardin Zoologique et Hôpital Psychiatrique," in A.
Brion and Henri Ey, eds., *Psychiatrie animale* (Paris, 1965), pp. 559–578.
Translated by Joseph and Barrie Klaits. Reprinted by permission of the
author and Editions Desclée de Brouwer.

1. Georges-Louis Leclerc, comte de Buffon, "Discours sur la nature des ani-
maux," in *Histoire naturelle* (Paris: Imprimerie Royale, 1753), 4: 3.

languishes in shameful captivity. The other, which might be called the zoomorphic fallacy, is not uncommon among certain behaviorist psychologists. One such psychologist, for example, after studying frustration phenomena in white rats, applied his findings directly to problems of international politics.

We will try to keep a safe distance from these two pitfalls. We are perfectly aware of the enormous gap which separates human nature from animal nature, but we also know that there are common denominators. It is from this viewpoint that we want to consider whether the study of psychological and psychopathic reactions of the animal in the zoological garden can help us better understand certain forms of human behavior in a closed environment, specifically the behavior of the mentally ill in psychiatric institutions.

HISTORY OF THE ZOOLOGICAL GARDEN

The history of the zoological garden has been treated definitively by Gustave Loisel[2] in a richly illustrated work of encyclopedic documentation from which we have extracted a large part of what follows. Loisel showed that the zoological garden is considerably older than is generally believed and that it has played an important role in the history of culture. Five periods can be distinguished.

I. Prehistoric Period

Galton held that long before they thought of domestication, men captured and kept young animals for simple pleasure, not for a practical purpose. When large tribes appeared, their chief-

2. Gustave Loisel, *Histoire des ménageries de l'antiquité à nos jours,* 3 vols. (Paris: Doin et Laurens, 1912).

tains sometimes established collections of wild animals. . . .[3]
Later in the evolution of human society there appeared the
great empires of Assyria and Babylonia, and the menagerie of
tribal chieftains became the *paradeisos*.

II. Period of the Paradeisos

The Persian word *paradeisos* referred to a very large walled
park, where numerous beasts were kept in conditions of relative liberty for the monarch's pleasure. Many of these animals
were no doubt tame. The *paradeisos* served multiple functions.
Animals presented to the king were held there, as were those
intended as gifts for his friends. The *paradeisos* furnished animals for the royal hunts, for ceremonial processions, and also
probably as models for court artists. Finally, it is possible that
the *paradeisos* had a mystical function: the king, incarnation of
the divine, received animal homage to the master of creation
in a garden closed to common mortals.

It was in ancient Persia that the institution of the *paradeisos*
reached its apogee.[4] The biblical Garden of Eden is but an
idealized image of the Persian *paradeisos*, which, according to
the Hebrew prophets, became the "paradise" promised to re-
generated humanity, where the lion and the lamb were to live
peacefully side by side.

Also from Persia came the first indication of a scientific contribution by the zoological garden. Pliny recounts that Alexander,
after his victory over Darius, sent Aristotle animals that he had
captured all over the Persian empire. More likely these animals
were rounded up in one of the *paradeisos* of the Great King.

---

3. Francis Galton, "Domestication of Animals," in *Inquiries into Human
Faculty* (1865; reprinted London: Dent, 1911), pp. 173–194.
4. The remains of a *paradeisos* were discovered in Syria in 1900. Cf. Cler-
mont-Ganneau, *Le paradeisos royal achéménide de Sidon*, Académie des In-
scriptions (Paris), session of December 17, 1920.

The Greeks apparently never maintained animal parks. By contrast, in Rome there was the *vivarium* where merchants housed animals destined for the cruel games of the Colosseum. After the fall of the Persian empire, the tradition of the *paradeisos* survived in India and China, and Loisel found relics of them on the Indian subcontinent and in Thailand.

III. Period of the "Menageries"

In the Middle Ages, kings and noblemen often kept wild beasts in their palace or castle. Some towns had bear pits or a "lion house." Here and there a new type of zoological garden appeared, the "menagerie," in which animals, grouped approximately by genus or species, lived in cages or separate enclosures. According to Loisel, the oldest known example was located on the grounds of the eleventh-century St. Gall monastery. There animals were systematically grouped and classified in "a peculiar, cell-like system of division."

However, as Loisel stressed, "for a long time the only true zoological garden in the world was that of the Aztecs of Mexico, which was destroyed by the Spaniards." We know of it thanks to the accounts of the conquistadores and from a letter by Cortez to Charles V, dated October 30, 1520, from which comes this excerpt:

Apart from this castle which he inherited from his ancestors, Lord Montezuma possesses another which he built himself. It is made of marble, richly decorated with jasper, with a magnificent pleasure garden in which there are ten pools of water inhabited by aquatic birds, all tame. Some of these pools are filled with salt water, since they are used for sea birds. The birds receive food appropriate to their species. Worm eaters are fed worms, the corn eaters corn, and fish eaters fish. Some three hundred keepers, who have no other occupation, watch over these birds. The animals even have physicians. . . .

In one particularly large and beautiful house are kept many species of birds of prey, in cages one and a half times the height of a man and measuring six feet wide and long. The ceiling and the lower half of the walls are stone, the upper half woven reeds; at night and when it rains they nestle in sheltered corners. They are fed poultry.

On the first floor of the same building there are long halls adorned with grillwork cages carved in solid wood, and inside, lions, tigers, wolves, foxes and cats of every species, all in great number. They too are fed poultry and are cared for by three hundred keepers.

In another house live dwarves, hunchbacks, and all sorts of other monstrosities and deformities, men and women, each in a separate room. They too have their guards. There are also strange creatures, men, women and children, who from birth have faces, bodies, hair, eyelashes and eyebrows that are completely white.

Apart from its original purposes of providing luxury, ornament, and amusement for the king and his court, this huge menagerie furnished animals for royal hunts and for certain sacrifices, and supplied workshops making fur clothing and feather products; it also provided models for animal sculptors and jewelers, and some of the dead animals went to the taxidermist to be conserved.

In addition to this menagerie situated in the royal capital, Tenochtitlán (Mexico City), there was another in Tézcuco, the scientific center of the empire. A library and a museum of natural history adjoined it, as well as "a large hall and several chambers where historians, priests, and philosophers of the realm met and worked." The destruction of this institution with its library and of the menagerie of Tenochtitlán constitutes a deplorable loss to humanity. At least three centuries passed, said Loisel, before there appeared in Europe a zoo of a caliber equivalent to that of Tenochtitlán-Mexico City.

In his curious work *The New Atlantis*,[5] written between 1614 and 1617, Francis Bacon described an imaginary land where

5. Francis Bacon, *The New Atlantis*, Great Books of the Western World, no. 30 (Chicago: Encyclopaedia Britannica, 1952), pp. 199–214.

life was dominated by the cult of scientific research. The parks there contained specimens of all the known animals, which were used in experiments in physiotherapy, including the fabrication of monsters, hybrids, and new species. Here was the foreshadowing of a new trend: the utilization of the zoo for scientific research.

It was in France that this new kind of establishment saw the light of day. In 1662 Louis XIV created the Menagerie of Versailles, intended from the outset to be the biggest and most magnificent in the world. Although this was primarily a display establishment reserved for the visits of the king and the court in full ceremonial, Louis XIV also made it a research center. Upon arrival each animal was painted or represented in miniature by a known artist. Scientific exploitation of the menagerie was placed in the hands of the Académie des Sciences, whose members did many animal dissections and produced the first important work in comparative anatomy. Loisel tells the famous story of the ceremonial dissection of an elephant in 1681, an event which the Sun King deigned to honor with his presence: "Never perhaps was there a more imposing anatomical dissection, judged by the enormity of the animal, by the precision with which its several parts were examined, or by the quality and number of assistants." But Loisel also rendered the sad account of the decline of the menagerie under Louis XV and Louis XVI and its inglorious end during the Revolution.

IV. Period of the Classical "Zoo"

The era of the French Revolution inaugurated a new conception of the zoological garden. Until that time menageries, even those such as Versailles' where important scientific work was done, served primarily as diversions for the monarch and his courtiers. This is why the Encyclopedia declared: "Menageries must be destroyed when people have no bread, for it is scandal-

ous for animals to feast while around them men starve."
Whence followed the destruction of the menagerie of Versailles
by the revolutionaries. Bernardin de Saint-Pierre had the remnants of the menagerie transported to the Paris Jardin du Roi,
of which he was intendant, and proposed the creation of a new
institution. A report on this subject was prepared by three
members of the Natural History Society of Paris, Brongniart,
Millin, and Philippe Pinel. One would like to know just how
much Pinel, the famous alienist, contributed to the report of
1792, which concluded: "A menagerie like those that princes
and kings are accustomed to maintain is nothing but a costly
and unnecessary imitation of Asiatic pomp; but we think that a
menagerie without frills could be extremely useful to natural
history, to physiology and to the economy." The new institution
would serve both scientific progress and public instruction.
Thus was created, in the rebaptized Jardin des Plantes, the
National Menagerie of the Museum of Natural History in Paris,
the zoo that served as a model for all similar institutions
throughout the nineteenth century. There one of its first direc-
tors, Frédéric Cuvier (brother of the more famous zoologist
Georges Cuvier), made numerous pioneering and unjustly neglected observations of animal psychology.

The nineteenth century was the century of the classical zoological garden, the zoo where animals lived side by side in barred
cages or in little rustic chalets and miniscule enclosures. In
imitation of the Parisian model, there sprang up the zoos of
London (1829), Amsterdam (1838), Berlin (1844), Antwerp
(1848), and many others. Some were financed by national or
municipal governments, others by a zoological society (as was
the London zoo), still others were private commercial enter-
prises. In every great city the Sunday outing at the zoo,
crowded with curiosity seekers rubbing shoulders and gaping at
elephants, lions, and monkeys, became one of the features of
popular life. Among the visitors were numerous artists and

scientists; Darwin and Galton were said to have frequented the London zoo.

V. Period of the Modern Zoological Garden

This new period was inaugurated in Germany by the famous wild-animal dealer Carl Hagenbeck (1844–1913).[6] Hagenbeck's father had furnished animals for circuses and menageries, and the son transformed this modest trade into a huge enterprise involving expeditions to every corner of the world. In 1907 Hagenbeck and the Swiss architect and sculptor Urs Eggenschwyler constructed at Stellingen, just outside Hamburg, an immense park where animals were separated from the public not by bars but by deep, barely visible moats. The animals had ample space to roam, and the intention was to re-create their natural habitat as closely as possible. Hagenbeck was not only a businessman of genius but knowledgeable in animal psychology, as is indicated by his founding a school for animal trainers.

Hagenbeck's innovations were adopted by many zoological gardens. The first result was an improvement in the biological condition of animals. Many species that had never reproduced in captivity began to do so in modern zoos. Meanwhile, more and more attention was directed toward psychological troubles due to captivity. Frédéric Cuvier had already called attention to "the characteristic stupor which one observes among the inhabitants of certain menageries."[7] Darwin noted that circus lions reproduced more readily than caged lions in zoos and thought that the psychic stimulation experienced by the circus animal might play a role.[8] Loisel in 1912 devoted several pages

6. Carl Hagenbeck wrote an interesting autobiography, *Von Tieren und Menschen* (1908; reprinted Munich: List-Verlag, 1954).
7. Cited by Loisel with an inexact reference.
8. Charles Darwin, *The Variations of Animals and Plants under Domestication* (1868), vol. 2, chap. 18.

of his great work to the urgent need of numerous and varied psychological stimuli for zoo animals. But it is only in our time that the study of animal psychology and psychopathology in the zoological garden has flourished; and in this Hediger has been one of the main pioneers.[9]

Progress in animal psychology has permitted us to better comprehend certain basic characteristics of human nature, to determine what is innate and what is transmitted by culture,[10] and even to sketch—as Frauchiger did[11]—a comparative psychopathology for man and animals. As we showed in 1953,[12] it has become legitimate to attempt a comparison between symptoms brought about in animals by captivity and in man by a prolonged stay in a psychiatric hospital.

GENERAL COMPARISON

A general comparison of the zoological garden with the psychiatric hospital must consider the fact that each of these two institutions has undergone its own series of metamorphoses. We have seen how the *paradeisos,* where the animals lived in freedom, was replaced by the menagerie, where animals were caged; how the princely private menagerie was succeeded by the public zoo of the nineteenth century and then by the modern zoological park, a place to observe animal psychology. The forerunners of the psychiatric hospital are much less ancient,

9. H. Hediger, *Wildtiere in Gefangenschaft* (Basel: Benno Schwabe, 1942); see also his other publications.

10. Rousseau erred when he wrote, "The first man who put up a fence and declared, 'this field is mine' is the inventor of property." The feeling of ownership of individual "territory" is basic in the animal. Cf. M. Meyer-Holzapfel, *Die Bedeutung des Besitzes bei Tier und Mensch* (Bienne: Institut für Psycho-Hygiene, 1952).

11. E. Frauchiger, *Seelische Erkrankungen bei Mensch und Tier* (Bern: Hans Huber, 1945; 2d ed., 1953).

12. *L'évolution psychiatrique,* no. 2 (1953): 315–318.

even if one goes back to the Byzantine *morotrophion* of the fifth century and the Arab *moristan* of the Middle Ages, from which were perhaps derived the first Spanish insane asylums of the fifteenth century, the true ancestors of our present psychiatric hospitals.

Yet even given these transformations, one can identify permanent features, and sometimes identical ones, characteristic of both the zoo and the psychiatric hospital. Among the identical patterns we observe first a similarity of structure which may be summarized as follows:

ZOOLOGICAL GARDEN		PSYCHIATRIC ESTABLISHMENTS	
Authorities -	Zoologists	Authorities -	Psychiatrists
	Keepers		Attendants
(Public) -	Animals	(Public) -	Patients

We put the word "public" in parentheses to denote the area in which historical changes have been most marked. We have seen that for many centuries zoological gardens were reserved for the privileged few, while today they are open to all. The reverse has been the case for the psychiatric institution. In the seventeenth and eighteenth centuries, many asylums were open to the public, to be visited exactly as zoos are today. It was not until the nineteenth century that they became hermetically sealed. Thus the most instructive comparison would be of the "madhouse" of the seventeenth century and the contemporary open zoo.

In fact, the residents of these two kinds of institutions shared the singular characteristic of attracting upon themselves the hostile, aggressive, and cruel reactions of the public. The casual visitor to the zoo perhaps does not notice this, but the keepers are well aware of what happens when they relax their attention. Here, for example, is the account of a former keeper at the Moscow Zoo, Vera Hégi:[13]

[Among the spectators] crept hordes of the embittered, discontented with the world and with themselves, accompanied everywhere with their rancors and their deceptions. Under the pretext of getting their money's worth they would wake up sleeping lions with a blow of their canes, or insist that the bears perform stunts for the miserable reward of a fistful of food. . . .

All day long a huge, annoying and rowdy crowd paraded before the cages. This crowd, which would have been panic-stricken by the sight of a single one of these beasts uncaged, delighted in seeing them so disarmed, humiliated and debased. The mob avenged its own cowardice with boorish calls and shakes of the animals' chains, while the keepers' protests were countered by the incontestable reply, "I paid for it."

Compare this account with the picture of Bedlam Hospital in London revealed by historical research:

On each side of the gate there was a column capped by a statue of Madness personified by a grimacing head, as today a carved elephant might decorate the entrance to a zoo.[14] According to Robert Reed[15] a Sunday visit to Bedlam was one of London's great amusements. It has been calculated that during most of the eighteenth century Bedlam received an average of three hundred visitors a day. They entered through "penny gates," so-called because the admission charge was a penny. The sums paid by visitors constituted one of the asylum's most important sources of revenue. The visitor, after checking his sword in the vestibule, had the right to wander through all the wings, look in all the cells, speak to the patients and make fun of them. In exchange for their rejoiners, he might give the patients something to eat, or he might give them alcohol to stimulate them further. A Hogarth print shows a degenerate terminating a career of vice in Bedlam, chained

13. Vera Hégi, *Les captifs du zoo* (Lausanne: Spes, 1942), pp. 8, 13.
14. Daniel Hack Tuke, *Chapters in the History of the Insane in the British Islands* (London: Kegan Paul, 1882), pp. 69–79.
15. Robert Reed, *Bedlam on the Jacobean Stage* (Cambridge, Mass.: Harvard University Press, 1952).

in a squalid cell while two elegant visitors look him over as if he were some curious beast. Probably the inmates of Bedlam seemed more agitated and more "mad" than our present-day patients.

These examples drawn from a notorious madhouse and from a modern zoo show the similarity of the public's instinctive attitudes toward the madman and the caged beast. Still we should not generalize, because this aggressive, hateful, and cruel streak appears in only a fraction of the public. The typical public attitude varies according to time and place. Vera Hégi's descriptions of the Moscow Zoo, for example, come from the time of the civil war; today visitors to the same zoo seem more friendly to the animals.[16] It would be useful to have in-depth studies of these cultural and chronological variations. In a remarkable work, J. Koty[17] has amassed a large source collection on the attitudes of primitive peoples toward the aged, the disabled, and the sick, including the mentally ill. It emerges that some peoples are kind and devoted toward the "useless mouths," while others are hard and cruel. The comparative attitude of diverse peoples toward animals has not yet apparently been the object of inquiry. This is a regrettable gap because it would be instructive to compare cultural attitudes toward animals and the mentally ill.

Let us recall that in the past a number of zoological gardens exhibited human specimens. Montezuma's zoo featured dwarves, hunchbacks, and albinos. Loisel cites several Italian Renaissance princes who maintained a collection of Negroes, Tartars, and Moors in addition to a menagerie. The famous "wild boy of Aveyron" was lodged in the Jardin des Plantes before Itard took him in. It was not so long ago that P. T.

16. At least this seems to be the lesson of a more recent book written by a keeper in the same zoo. Vera Chaplina, *Zoo Babies* (Moscow: Foreign Languages Publishing House, n.d.).

17. John Koty, *Die Behandlung der Alten und Kranken bei den Naturvölkern* (Stuttgart: Hirschfeld, 1934).

Barnum exhibited American Indians in his circus along with bears and tigers and that Hagenbeck exhibited groups of Lapps, Nubians, Patagonians, Hottentots, and so forth in his Stellingen zoo.[18]

We should also note that there was a certain parallelism between the reform of zoological gardens and that of psychiatric institutions. The creation of the menagerie at the Jardin des Plantes, ancestor of modern zoos, occurred simultaneously with reform of "madhouses." One should therefore not be surprised to see the name Pinel associated with both these movements. Again in the early nineteenth century, Hagenbeck invented the modern zoological park and a new system of taming and training wild animals; a few years later another German, Hermann Simon, introduced his "activity therapy" *(aktivere Therapie)* at Gütersloh, a therapy which has been justifiably compared to a method of intensive training for the chronically mentally ill. . . .

Now we shall take a closer look at the structure of the modern zoological garden, comparing it to that of the psychiatric hospital. . . .

On the psychiatric side, many studies have been devoted to the personality and vocation of the psychiatrist, . . . and the same is true for the attitudes and reactions of the nursing personnel. At the same time, we are beginning to distinguish the psychotic's symptoms from his "role" as patient and his inter-psychological reactions toward other patients, the attendants, and the doctors. We are not aware of similar research in the domain of the zoo. What are the motives, conscious or unconscious, that lead someone to become the director of a zoo or an animal keeper? How are relationships among humans struc-

18. An English novelist invented the story of a man who volunteers to represent the human species in the monkey cage of a zoo. This novel is less fantastical than its author perhaps believed. Cf. David Garnett; *A Man in the Zoo* (London: Chatto & Windus, 1924).

tured in the zoo, and what are their effects on the psychological condition of the animals? In the absence of scientific studies, the only document we have found on this subject is Vera Hégi's book, which contains a remarkable gallery of psychological portraits of keepers and furnishes informative details about the interior life of the zoo—its intrigues and rumors, its legends or traditional history as transmitted orally from keeper to keeper, and so on. The picture this book provides of the zoo is that of an intricate web of relationships—man to man, man to animal, and animal to animal. One example is the author's account of an elk's assault on its keeper. Here we see interplays among (a) the attacking elk's jealousy of a young elk that the keeper tended, (b) the personal rancor of the elk for the keeper, who had ceased offering him a daily caress, (c) a conflict between two keepers. Is it not remarkable that aggression was produced at the critical moment of conflict between the two keepers, much as the studies of Stanton and Schwartz[19] have shown a relationship between the agitation of a mental patient and the conflicts of their attendants?

Let us now consider the perspective through which the residents of the two types of institutions are viewed by the human beings who surround them. We all know how differently a given mental patient can be judged by his doctor and by his attendant. A psychiatrist will be attracted by the scientific interest of a "rare case" or by the patient who might be cured by a new kind of therapy. An attendant is interested mainly in the quiet, submissive, and obliging "good patient" or in the one who provides a sense of fulfillment, as is typified by the eagerness of young nurses to busy themselves with insulin treatments instead of caring for the old and senile. As for the public, we know that in Bedlam the visitors distinguished a few "stars" or favor-

19. A. Stanton and M. Schwartz, "The Management of a Type of Institutional Participation in Mental Illness," *Psychiatry* 12 (1949): 13–26.

ite patients from the majority of dull residents. Who were these stars? We can guess by seeing which patients today are most striking to the casual visitor at one of our hospitals: the maniac who laughs and says funny things, the paranoid who believes himself to be Jesus Christ, and so forth.

We are assured that in the zoological garden there are similar differences between the viewpoints of the zoologist, the keeper and the public. The zoologist is most interested in rare animals like the okapi and Sumatran rhinoceros, or in the young of a species that rarely reproduces in captivity. The keeper will prefer the animal that is both docile and loved by the public. As for the visitors, animal exhibitors have long known that their reactions are dominated by irrational and paradoxical factors. The director of a famous circus became indignant when not a half-dozen visitors looked at a rhinoceros that had cost him twelve thousand dollars, while throngs crowded in front of a group of monkeys worth forty-five dollars.[20] Indeed, the success of animals with the public—and consequently the financial success of the zoo—depends upon a most intriguing factor: the "exhibition value" *(Schauwert)*, which represents a complex phenomenon of man-animal interpsychology.

Hediger has given us an excellent study of exhibition value.[21] This value has nothing to do with the animal's commercial worth or its utility to man, even less with its rarity or its scientific value. The public will mistake an okapi for an old mule and will not distinguish the rarest Sumatran rhinoceros for an ordinary African one. According to Hediger, the animals with the gift of attracting public favor belong to a few well-defined groups: (a) the traditional "exotic animal" (elephant, camel, giraffe); (b) the big cats (lion, tiger, leopard); (c) the large snakes;

20. William Mann, *Wild Animals in and out of the Zoo*, Smithsonian Scientific Series (New York, 1930), p. 45.
21. H. Hediger, "Vom Schauwert der Tiere," *Atlantis* (August 1955), pp. 348–352.

(d) the agile and active animal who performs tricks, begs, and "works with" the public; (e) all baby animals and small varieties of other animals (so that the pony will be preferred to a horse); (f) the monkeys, bears, penguins, and all animals that stand upright. Wouldn't this last category be that of animals capable of inspiring kinesthetic images in Rorschach's sense?

Apart from these general public reactions there are more specific ones. Certain zoo habitués are attracted by the sexual life of the monkeys. Hediger writes that "these specialists are generally well known to the keepers, who label them with nicknames, and they are often placed under a surveillance much tighter than they might suspect." But in general the attraction exercised by monkeys upon the public seems much more complex. Some visitors probably experience a sort of morose pleasure in considering the resemblance of the monkey to man—a degraded and debased man, analogous to the erstwhile madmen of Bedlam. One might also conjecture upon the fact that the sight of monkeys gesturing and grimacing produces a blossoming of kinesthetic images in man. We recall in this regard that Hermann Rorschach, while still a young intern at Münsterlingen, began to study the effects upon the mentally ill of the sight of a monkey.[22] One of my friends once took a mute negative catatonic for an outing in a zoo. The catatonic had no reaction to the sight of animals except that when she saw the monkeys she laughed without uttering a word. This test was not repeated because the patient attracted too much public attention, to the detriment of the animals. It is lamentable that no one has resumed Rorschach's studies of the reactions of the mentally ill toward monkeys, and vice versa.

As for the large carnivores, visitors regard them with a sort of sado-masochistic shudder at the thought that these beasts would fall upon people and devour them were it not for the

22. H. Ellenberger, "The Life and Work of Hermann Rorschach," *Bulletin of the Menninger Clinc* 18 (1954): 173–219, especially 192, 197.

cages and bars. The public is mad about the sight of lions devouring large chunks of bloody meat, which obliges the zoo
management to feed these animals once a day even though in
the wild they eat once a week at most. But this is precisely the
source of their exhibition value, the essential factor for the
prosperity of the zoo. Can we help but see in the popularity of
the carnivores' dinner a distant reflection of the bloodlust that
stimulated the Romans in seeing the condemned devoured in
the circus?[23]

If monkeys represent for some a form of degraded humanity,
and the lions an incarnation of elemental and brutal passions,
the prestige of the snakes is in an entirely different class. A man
can project his feelings upon a lion, so that a tamer is able to
establish an affective rapport with the beast; but however skill-
ful the snake charmer he only makes use of certain reflexes of
the reptile and establishes no more than an uncertain psychological relationship with it. The psychic reactions produced in
man by the snake take place mostly on the unconscious level.
The snake intrigues us by its psychic activity with which no
Einfühlung, no empathy, is possible; and what renders it even
more frightening is that while it can be directed toward certain
specific ends it remains very dangerous. It is not surprising that
many zoo visitors avoid the reptile house, while others are fascinated by the snakes, especially in the zoos where the public
is admitted to watch them eat. Galton[24] has given a good description of public reactions to this spectacle:

Rabbits, birds, and other small animals were dropped in the different
cages, which the snakes, after more or less serpentine action, finally
struck with their poison fangs or crushed in their folds. I found it a

23. Vera Hégi, in her account "How Five Tigers Killed Their Keeper," says
that this drama brought the animals "a prodigious popularity because the public
is always avid to contemplate a beast who sheds human blood." Cf. *Les captifs
du zoo,* pp. 126–137.
24. F. Galton, "Character," in *Inquiries into Human Faculty* (London: Dent,
1907), p. 40.

horrible but a fascinating scene. . . . This exhibition of the snakes at their feeding-time, which gave to me, as it doubtless did to several others, a sense of curdling of the blood, had no such effect on many of the visitors. I have often seen people—nurses, for instance, and children of all ages—looking unconcernedly and amusedly at the scene. Their indifference was perhaps the most painful element of the whole transaction. Their sympathies were absolutely unawakened.

The height of horror is presented by the spectacle of a python or any other giant serpent devouring a living pig or kid.[25] Here the "sado-masochistic shudder" is undoubtedly of an entirely different character from that elicited by the lions' meals.

Only a small number of zoo visitors are not content with contemplative emotions and indulge in criminal attacks upon the animals. There is hardly a work on zoos that does not contain ample documentation on this subject and the following memories of Vera Hégi are an example:

Every kind of perverse baseness found among the scum of a large city gathers in the zoological garden. Foiling the most vigilant surveillance, visitors manage to throw all sorts of filthy things—stones, lighted matches, pieces of broken glass—into the mouths of the animals. Or by spitting into the animals' mouths, they transmit their tuberculosis or other contagious diseases; in this way, for example, we have lost dozens of monkeys. [Accounts follow of animals poisoned or killed by needles given by the public.] It would not be at all surprising if most of our old keepers ended up hardened misanthropes who considered the public their mortal enemy.[26]

These cruel attempts upon the lives of animals constitute an underdeveloped area of criminology, but they also inspire us to

25. "Each time it was an atrociously distressing scene. . . . At first the little animal didn't understand what was expected of her and began to play with the monster. When the latter, in a single bound, pounced upon her and tried unsuccessfully to swallow her up, the victim, badly bitten and covered with blood, struggled and uttered hideous cries. . . ." Hégi, *Les captifs du zoo*, pp. 115–116.

26. *Ibid.*, p. 9.

reflect upon the conditions of the mentally ill. Historical records show that in the seventeenth and eighteenth centuries such people were not only displayed before a hostile and mocking public, not only chained and whipped under the pretext of treatment, but often also maltreated by any passerby. The famous Father Surin, during the course of his attack of depression, was once visited by an ecclesiastic who contemplated him in silence for half an hour, suddenly slapped him, and then left without a word.[27] The history of witchcraft trials abounds with examples of clearly insane individuals who were tortured and died at the stake.[28] It would be oversimplistic to explain these events merely as the results of ignorance, fanaticism, or collective hysteria on the part of the judges; one must add to these the activation of latent aggressive tendencies in the presence of the mentally ill, or perhaps of certain types of mentally ill who need to be more precisely defined.

To return to the zoo public, we mention a final category, that of "animal protectors." There is no impulse more virtuous than the sentiment that prompts generous souls to ameliorate the lot of maltreated animals. Unfortunately, too many alleged friends of animals are motivated by confused feelings, if not by a reverse sadism.[29] Not many years ago in Topeka, Kansas, a "humanitarian" society lodged a complaint against the director of the municipal zoo who, they charged, was starving the lions: the poor animals "were nothing but skin and bones." An expert's report concluded that those lions were in excellent health and were at optimum weight for their age. . . . There were undoubtedly three motives for the friends of the lions in Topeka: (a)

27. Cited by Aldous Huxley, *The Devils of Loudun* (New York: Harper & Row, 1952).

28. Cf. Mönkemöller, "Tortur und Geisteskrankheit," *Allgemeine Zeitschrift für Psychiatrie* 61 (1904): 58–107.

29. See the story of the "intolerable benefactress" and other events reported by Hégi.

projection upon the lions of a complex of endured injustices; (b) their ignorance of zoology, which made them think the ideal normal lion was the typical unhealthy and obese menagerie lion; (c) the quasi-mythical prestige of the lion as "king of the beasts" and "lord of the jungle." We should also mention that another group of Topeka animal lovers once serenaded the lions with carols on Christmas Eve. Why lions rather than hyenas or jackals? In answer, consider the lion's image in the popular mind: he comprises the archetype of the heroic male virtues (whereas in reality the male lion lives in indolence while the female does the hunting).

The reactions of visitors to zoo animals have little to do with zoology. They are thoroughly irrational and express obscure impulses the study of which has hardly begun. Very likely the same complexity obtains in the domain of the instinctive reactions of the average man toward the insane. A rational and humane attitude toward animals as well as toward the mentally ill can only be the fruit of long and persistent individual and collective education.

What are the animals' reactions to their visitors? These reactions vary among species and among individuals within species. An especially important factor is the duration of captivity. Hediger has shown how traumatizing the presence of man can be for the newly captured wild animal. . . . Produced in the animal are anxiety, agitation, and nervous activity. Ernest Inhelder[30] published the case history of a hyena whose intense nervous activity diminished markedly when the space separating him from the public was increased from three to six meters. Over time this distance could be progressively reduced.

For an animal accustomed to captivity, by contrast, the presence of the public is an indispensable psychic stimulant. In his classic work,[31] Loisel showed that animals kept too far from the

30. Ernest Inhelder, "Zur Psychologie einiger Verhaltensweisen—besonders des Spiels—von Zootieren," *Zeitschrift für Tierpsychologie* 12 (1955): 88–144.
31. Loisel, *Histoire des ménageries,* 3: 386–387.

public became slow, unhappy, and sickly, while those in direct contact were active, gay, and lively. A glance at the large mammals and many birds in a zoo is enough to show how much they enjoy being admired by the public and how well some of them know how to play their "role." Grzimek has maintained that this is mutual exhibitionism in which it is often the human who tries to attract the animals' attention.[32]

Returning to the psychiatric hospital, do we not observe a similar situation among the mentally ill? In cases of acute psychosis there is the same intolerance of human presence, the same "presence reactions" (Baruk). In chronic cases, by contrast, we know only too well in what states of private stupor, pseudodementia, and alienation patients confined in isolated cells used to founder. Odious as was the system at Bedlam, it at least had the advantage of furnishing constant psychic stimulation to the patients, and this treatment cured more often than did the deadly cell system of the nineteenth century.

These considerations apply to another psychohygienic factor: work. It has long been known that the ambulant animal in the circus or menagerie did better than the animal of the classical zoo. As Hediger[33] has shown, this is not only the result of better physiological hygiene but also and especially because the work done by the circus animal provides a psychological stimulant. Its role might be compared to that of physical therapy for the mental patient.

COMPARATIVE PSYCHOPATHOLOGICAL SYNDROMES

Psychopathological symptoms attributable to a prolonged stay in a closed environment have been observed in a variety

32. B. Grzimek, "Gefangenhaltung von Tieren," *Studium Generale* 3 (1950): 1–5.
33. H. Hediger, "Ergebnisse tierpsychologischer Forschung im Zirkus," *Die Naturwissenschaften* 26 (1938): 242–252.

of settings, including prisons, civil or military internment camps, orphanages, tuberculosis sanatoria, psychiatric hospitals, and so on.[34] Zoological gardens are no exception, and a variety of such syndromes have been described in animals. We shall choose the cases that lend themselves best to parallels with human psychiatry.

It goes without saying that such a comparison cannot be made indiscriminately, because of the differences between man and animal and among animal species. Even among animals of the same species reactions depend upon an individual's previous experiences.

Let us consider, for example, five zoo lions: one, captured in the bush as an adult, remains incurably stamped by the trauma of captivity; a second, captured very young, successfully adapts to his new life; the third, born in the zoo, never knew another milieu; a fourth, also born in captivity but raised as a cub by masters who fondled and pampered him; and a fifth, who came from a circus where he had been trained and had led an active and eventful life. It is obvious that these five animals, identical to the casual observer, represent very different cases from the psychological point of view.

I. The Trauma of Captivity

Carl Hagenbeck did an excellent study of the intense disturbances affecting the newly captured animal. Often the capture had been preceded by a long pursuit. The exhausted animal might have died of cardiac collapse or pulmonary inflammation but for emergency resuscitation treatments. Hagenbeck, who devised a system for treating these disorders, contended that it was useless to think of the animal's adjustment to captivity while he was still affected by this trauma.

34. H. Ellenberger, "Zoological Garden and Mental Hospital," *Canadian Psychiatric Association Journal* 5 (1960): 136–149.

Hediger[35] thinks that the trauma of captivity is primarily psychic, resulting from the sudden change in mode of life. In its native habitat the animal is narrowly integrated into a space-time system which includes its individual or collective "territory" and its biorhythms. The animal is also part of a social system in which group relations are thoroughly regulated even to the smallest details. The animal uprooted from these systems, as well as from his *Umwelt*, is completely disoriented. Furthermore, as we have noted above, the captive animal finds himself in constant proximity to his mortal enemy, man, and can neither escape nor attack.[36] In this situation, according to Hediger, the animal can react in one of three ways: (a) attacks of acute agitation, at times extraordinarily violent, and often resulting in severe wounds such as cranial fractures, or even death; (b) a prolonged stupor; (c) a kind of hunger strike, which can result in the animal's death if it is not forcibly fed.

According to Hediger the trauma of captivity dominates the whole psychopathology of zoo animals. It increases in severity with the age of the animal. Shepstone[37] affirms that the elephant is the only wild mammal that can long survive if captured as an adult. For the animal born in the zoo, this syndrome appears in attenuated form upon transfer from one institution to another.

We can recognize in the mentally ill a comparable syndrome, the "trauma of commitment." Here is a case history:

A thirty-year-old man from Texas, married and father of a small child, experienced troubles of a schizophrenic nature over two or three years. His family decided to have him committed to a mental hospital.

35. H. Hediger, "Freiheit und Gefangenschaft im Leben des Tieres," *Ciba-Zeitschrift* 5, no. 54 (1938): 1850–1861.
36. We recall here that the very sight of the natural "mortal enemy" can induce serious mishaps. Rabbits placed in the presence of ferrets, even though separated from them, have been known to succumb to psychogenic death.
37. Harold Shepstone, *Wild Beasts Today* (London: Sampson Low, n.d.), p. 46.

He was taken to see his brother-in-law, a surgeon, under the pretext of having a blood test, which in reality was an intravenous injection with a powerful sedative. A waiting ambulance took the patient to the airport, where a plane, also hired in advance, took him to a city in Kansas where his commitment to an institution had been prearranged. When the patient finally regained consciousness, he discovered that he was in a "madhouse" a thousand miles from home and that his family already had gone back by plane. For several years the mental attitude of this patient was completely dominated by the shock of what he called—not without reason—his "kidnapping." His rage against his wife, his brother-in-law, and the psychiatrists, whom he erroneously regarded as accomplices in the ambush, was manifested in delusional ideas of persecution which dominated his morbid state much more than the mental disturbances preceding his commitment.

This is, fortunately, an exceptional case, but for many patients the circumstances of commitment, the transportation to the hospital, and the upsetting of daily routines constitute a serious and enduring shock, symptoms of which may be confused with those of the initial illness.

II. The Nestling Process

Once the zoo animal has overcome the effects of the first shock, a long and difficult process of adaptation begins. The animal, dispossessed of his natural "territory," must grow to appropriate his cage or his zoo enclosure and to make it his new "territory." This is the essential event which will make other adaptations possible. As an example, here is an instance borrowed from Hediger:[38]

The tiger Griedo, bought from the zoo in Philadelphia, arrived at the Zurich zoo on April 9, 1957. He was to be mated with the tigress Fatma. But Griedo was upset, stayed in a corner of his cage, was shy

38. H. Hediger in *Neue Zürcher Zeitung*, March 16, 1958.

toward his keeper and not at all interested in Fatma. On June 25, 1957, two and a half months after his arrival, the tiger made his "proprietor's tour" of his cage, the periphery of which he "marked" with squirts of urine, in the same way a tiger in the wild marks the limits of his individual territory. The next day there was a remarkable change in the animal. He felt at home, his attitude toward the tigress also underwent a change, and as a result, some months afterwards Fatma brought a new little tiger into the world.

Such a change produces multiple effects. In the first place, since the prison has been transformed into individual territory, the animal no longer tries to escape. Mannteufel[39] has pointed out that some animals could easily leap over the barriers of their enclosures or demolish the walls of their shelters if they wished. But the barriers often serve more to protect the animals from the public than the other way around. Many animals refuse to leave their cages even when we try to make them come out; almost every book on zoos has stories of runaway animals who return of their own volition.

Mannteufel tells of a she-wolf from the Moscow Zoo who was taken in a taxi to an institution located on the opposite side of the city. Soon after arriving she escaped and, to the horror of the keepers, crossed the whole city, ran through crowds of people who took her for an Alsatian dog, and ended up at the zoo, where she bounded to the door of her cage.[40] Lorenz Hagenbeck recounts that during the bombing of Hamburg in June 1943, the Stellingen park was set on fire and many animals escaped. But all of them returned spontaneously or allowed themselves to be led back to their enclosures. The same thing happened, he adds, in all the other bombed German zoos.[41] As

39. P. Mannteufel, *Tales of a Naturalist* (Moscow: Foreign Languages Publishing House, n.d.), pp. 19–21.

40. *Ibid.*, pp. 49–50.

41. Lorenz Hagenbeck, *Den Tieren gehört mein Herz*, 2d ed. (Hamburg: O. J. Hoffman und Campe Verlag, 1955).

Grzimek put it, the animal who escapes from the zoo is not a prisoner who has regained his freedom, but a "displaced person" *(heimatlos)* generally eager to return "home" to his cage.[42]

When he has "taken possession" of his new "territory," the animal, often fearful until then, will defend it fiercely against all intruders. (From the human standpoint he becomes more "dangerous.") Some cases of aggression can be interpreted in this way. A deer will be very gentle as long as he is fed through the barrier but he becomes "nasty" to the imprudent person who would enter his enclosure.

Does not this basic process of taking possession of a place have a counterpart in the psychiatric hospital? The simplest form would be the nestling process, described and analyzed by Daumézon, whereby the cured patient remains attached to the asylum.[43] This is the condition of the recovered patient who refuses to leave the hospital and sometimes succeeds in spending the rest of his life there. Daumézon has unraveled the characteristic traits of the "nestling" patient: a passive individual, timid, submissive, single, often with no established occupation, and in a precarious economic situation. To the personnel he will be a "good" patient—docile, obliging, self-effacing, well-liked by all. But as soon as the eventuality of a discharge is mentioned his symptoms return, and it is by no means rare for such a patient to suffer a relapse just before his scheduled departure. If he is discharged, the patient does not wait long to return with a new certificate of commitment. In effect, this individual, whose social adaptation had been defective, finds in the asylum a milieu where he can be successfully integrated.

Analogous cases are found in other environments. Recently

42. Grzimek, "Gefangenhaltung von Tieren," pp. 1–5.
43. G. Daumézon, "L'enracinement des malades guéris à l'asile," *L'hygiène mentale* 36 (1946–47): 59–71.

some American authors, who were apparently unfamiliar with Daumézon's work, described a similar syndrome in military hospitals.[44] Hans Castorp, the hero of Thomas Mann's *The Magic Mountain,* was the prototype of this syndrome for the tuberculosis sanatorium. And cases of "nestling" prisoners are well known.

One interpretation of nestling is that the patient acquires a "territory" in the asylum. Expelled from it he is in the situation of the lion outside his cage who has nowhere to go but back in. The difference between the zoo and the psychiatric hospital is that in the former the process of taking possession is "normal," that is, desired and encouraged by the keepers, while in the psychiatric hospital nestling is considered abnormal so long as there is the slightest chance of recovery. . . .

III. Conflict and Social Rank

Animals can thrive only in an adequate social setting, balanced both in quantity (neither too many nor too few *socii*) and in quality (by a proper ratio of sexes, ages, and temperaments). These conditions cannot be met in most closed environments, which induce specific symptoms.

Overpopulation, a familiar problem in psychiatric hospitals, has been the subject of numerous administrative inquiries, but not, it would appear, of psychological studies. In the case of zoo animals, Ratcliffe[45] was able to show from autopsy statistics of the Philadelphia Zoo that the frequency of arteriosclerosis increased tenfold in mammals and twentyfold in birds between 1931 and 1956. This increase the author attributes to the in-

44. L. Gatto and H. Dean, "The 'Nestling' Military Patient," *Military Medicine* 117, no. 1 (1955): 1–26.

45. H. L. Ratcliffe and M. T. I. Cronin, "Changing Frequency of Arteriosclerosis in Mammals and Birds at the Philadelphia Zoological Garden," *Circulation* 18 (1958): 41–52.

86   HENRI F. ELLENBERGER

creased density of animal population, a generator of social pressures and of stress, which produce a dysfunction of the adrenal glands.

But more than a matter of numerical factors is involved here. Zoologists know that if you place an equal number of monkeys in several cages of the same dimensions, there will be terrible battles in some cages and none in others. Grzimek says that in a cage of baboons an excess of males will inevitably produce mortal combat, victimizing both sexes. Psychic equilibrium is optimal when the group consists of a small number of adult males, a larger number of females, and a group of young and infant animals.[46]

Further, the psychic health of an animal living in a zoo among his species depends to a large extent upon his "social rank." Schjelderup-Ebbe[47] and his followers have shown that in any group of mammals or birds a rigid social hierarchy is spontaneously established. At the top is a dominating "alpha animal" who takes his pick of food and resting place while demanding certain gestures and signs of submission from all the other animals. After him comes the second highest in rank, who acts in the same way toward all the others except the alpha animal, and so forth down the social ladder. At the bottom of the scale is the omega animal, a social pariah or underdog. The social rank often doubles as a hierarchy of mistreatment characterized by biting, clawing, pecking (the pecking order): the alpha animal mistreats all the others and no one touches him, the following animal is mistreated only by the alpha animal and mistreats all the others except the alpha animal, and so on, while the omega animal is the universal butt.

Now it appears that the pressure of social rank is more impla-

46. Grzimek, "Gefangenhaltun von Tieren," pp. 1–5.
47. Thorleif Schjelderup-Ebbe, "Beiträge zur Sozialpsychologie des Haushuhns," *Zeitschrift für Psychologie und Physiologie der Sinnesorgane* 88 (1922): 225–264.

cable in the zoological garden than in nature, as Grzimek[48] explains. Among baboons in the wild, the animal of low social rank creeps around the periphery of the group, hidden behind a tree and out of sight of the alpha animal. But in the restricted space of the monkey cage, where he cannot withdraw, he is deprived of food, tormented, bitten, and even killed. His situation is comparable to that of an honorable man imprisoned with hardened criminals. And, to be sure, there is nothing so similar to the animal system of social rank and pecking order than the spontaneous self-organization of convicts in a badly administered prison.

To the frustrations of intensified social ranking at the zoo are often added those created by the public or the keepers. When feeding the animals the public has no concern for their real needs but thinks only of their popularity. One sees visitors stuff young animals with delicacies, giving nothing to the adults in the same enclosure who perhaps need more to eat. Zoo keepers assure us that certain animals become sick with jealousy when they are fondled or admired less than animals in adjacent cages.

Do these data help us understand events observed in psychiatric hospitals? Probably more than we might suspect. The phenomena of social rank and social frustrations exist in the psychiatric hospital in a variety of forms. In some backward, poorly supervised institutions containing a large proportion of emotionally disturbed children we can see something like what exists in prisons: tyranny of the "leader," bullying of the weak, cruelty to those who resist. Furthermore, in some wards of schizophrenics there is social ranking of the patients in a primitive, attenuated form, as Balthasar Staehelin[49] has described. Most often, the situation is more complex, since a number of

48. Grzimek, "Gefangenhaltung von Tieren," pp. 1–5.
49. Balthasar Staehelin, "Gesetzmässigkeiten im Gemeinschaftsleben schwer Geisteskranker," *Schweizer Archiv für Neurologie und Psychiatrie* 72 (1953): 277–298.

factors intervene, including rivalry between old-timers and newcomers and the advantages of those with external support in the form of contacts with administrative personnel who confide others' secrets to them. In extreme cases such situations, when reinforced by the chance sympathies or antipathies of the personnel, seem to aggravate the loser of this social battle into delirium, hallucinations, and affective regression. This is Baruk's thesis in his "Psychiatrie morale."

Several procedures have been used to eliminate these pathogenic factors from the hospital environment. The great classical alienists knew the importance of the "ranking" of patients. They made daily observations of patients' interactions so as to separate or group them according to their reciprocal affinities. It is also important to eliminate as much as possible all injustices and social frustrations, as Baruk so aptly pointed out. Clearly, the more patients are submitted to a careful program of sociotherapy, the fewer manifestations there will be of "social rank" and other social frustrations.

IV. Emotional Deterioration

Emotional deterioration as a result of captivity has been extensively studied in the field of prison psychopathology. In mental hospitals it is much more difficult to recognize, because the physician has a natural tendency to confuse these with the clinical pattern of the disease proper. But Pinel pointed to this distinction long ago in exclaiming about mental patients who were fettered with irons: ". . . and how shall we distinguish between the disease and its aggravation [resulting from the chains]?" More recently, Hermann Simon proclaimed that many so-called catatonic symptoms were secondary products produced by pathogenetic factors in the hospital milieu. In fact, symptoms such as deep emotional regression and infantilism, pseudodementia and catatonic movements disappeared almost completely in institutions applying occupational therapy.

Symptoms of emotional deterioration in captive animals have been known at least since the time of Cuvier and Hagenbeck, but they have not been studied systematically until our time. According to Konrad Lorenz, species vary greatly in their tolerance of captivity. The lion is too lazy and the eagle too stupid to suffer very much. The worst off are very active animals like the wolf and fox, as well as intelligent animals like monkeys.[50] Among the environmental factors, two seem particularly harmful: limitation of movement in a confining cage or enclosure, and the lack of psychic stimulation, especially by isolation from the public.

Emotional deterioration can be diagnosed from a variety of symptoms, . . . including severe crises of anxiety, sudden bursts of aggression against their keepers or against others of their species, and self-destructive fits. Among these symptoms we will emphasize only two. The first is the repetitive movement executed by certain animals. Who has not seen in a zoo or touring menagerie a bear nodding his head or leaning from right to left, a tiger pacing in circles around his cage, a hyena making a figure 8, and so on? Hediger was the first to show that these repetitive movements were psychopathological reactions to captivity.[51] Then Dr. Meyer-Holzapfel did a systematic investigation of repetitious movements, analyzing their various etiological factors, including the tendency to habit formation, the role of sensory excitation, and the obstacles preventing satisfaction of normal needs. The most severe and difficult cases

50. K. Lorenz, *King Solomon's Ring* (1949; reprinted New York: Crowell, 1952).
51. H. Hediger, "Über Bewegungsstereotypien bei gehaltenen Tieren," *Revue suisse de zoologie* 41 (1934): 349–356.

are found among animals enclosed in very constricting places.[52]

The other symptom is coprophagia [that is, eating of excrement], which has been studied in chimpanzees and other large monkeys by Stemmler-Morath.[53] This too seems to be a phenomenon unknown in the wild and appears as a response to certain conditions of captivity. Sometimes it is brought about by an unbalanced diet, but more often there are psychic factors such as boredom and inactivity. This is why coprophagia (together with loss of usual cleaning habits) reappears among moneys in the winter when the animals do not have the distraction of people to look at and when bad weather precludes outdoor activity.

CONCLUSION

We are at a turning point in the history of the zoological garden as well as of the psychiatric hospital. Recent progress in therapy of the mentally ill makes one wonder if the psychiatric hospital will long survive in the form we know it or be replaced by institutions of a different characer. As for the zoological garden, the series of metamorphoses which have marked its history do not appear to have ceased.

In the past the zoo played an important cultural role. It is from the ancient *paradeisos* that humanity has derived several of its collective ideals, its philosophical and religious myths. Zoological gardens have contributed much to art and to natural science. Today they have become laboratories of animal and

52. M. Meyer-Holzapfel, "Die Entstehung einiger Bewegungsstereotypien bei gehaltenen Säugern und Vögeln," *Revue suisse de zoologie* 46 (1939) :567–580.
53. C. Stemmler-Morath, "Die Koprophagie, eine Gefangenschafterscheinung bei den Anthropomorphen," *Der Zoologische Garten* 9 (1937): 159–161.

comparative psychology. For several reasons their importance is likely to grow in the future.

Many of our contemporaries are still unaware of the immense tragedy that has been taking place in the last few decades. Man's unfeeling and senseless destruction of vast forests and other natural habitats has been followed by an alarming diminution of wild animal population. Many species will soon be extinct if radical measures are not taken soon.[54] The zoo might serve as a shelter for species threatened with extinction, and it might also help call public attention to the approaching catastrophe.

Further, the zoological garden becomes a more and more necessary corrective to the oppressive and destructive effects of our hypertechnological and hypermechanistic civilization.

Finally, as we witness the cultural unification of our planet, the ideals of Occident and Orient are being compared with greater accuracy. We are beginning to suspect that our Western culture has been too exclusively centered on man. Our spiritual ancestors, the Greeks and Romans, had almost no interest in nature and animals. It is significant that zoology, with the lone exception of Aristotle's work, was not treated scientifically in the West before modern times. The East, by contrast, never separated man from the rest of nature and from the unity of the living world. Perhaps there is in the Hindu respect for the sacred cow a deeper meaning than in the Cartesian beast-machine and in the dazzling work of our vivisectionists. German romanticism is the only Western movement in which we find a reflection of the Eastern view of the world and of animated nature.

In this regard it is intriguing that the most recent evolution of the zoological garden seems to mark a return toward the concept of the ancient *paradeisos.* A number of new zoological

54. B. Grzimek, *Kein Platz für wilde Tiere* (München: Kindler Verlag, 1950).

parks comprise large tracts where animals of different species roam freely, while visitors travel by car on marked paths. Mannteufel[55] reports that new conditioning procedures allow animals of enemy species to live in peace after being raised together. Will we one day see the revival of the Persian *paradeisos,* and will that revival produce a new ethical system?

55. Mannteufel, *Tales of a Naturalist.*

5.

The Civilized Animal

Joseph Wood Krutch

"There are many arguments, none of them very good, for having a snake in the house." So Mr. Will Cuppy once wrote, though he was gracious (or is it cynical?) enough to add: "Considering what some do pet, I don't see why they should draw the line at snakes."

Nevertheless one of my friends and neighbors has kept reptiles since he was seven years old and at this moment he has in his house a whole roomful, including some of the largest and most venomous of our native species. I have seen him stopped suddenly during a casual evening walk in the desert by a faint whir; seen him drop to the ground with a flashlight and then rise after a few seconds with a three-foot rattler held firmly and triumphantly just behind the head.

But it is some of his other pets—not of the sort to which Mr. Cuppy rather seems to be alluding—which concern me at the moment. The doorknob on his snake room is placed too high to be reached by his three children, of whom the eldest is now five, but he has reared free in the house two Arizona wildcats which,

SOURCE: Joseph Wood Krutch, *The Great Chain of Life*, pp. 129–144. Copyright ©1956 by Joseph Wood Krutch. Reprinted by permission of Houghton Mifflin Company.

until they got too big, the children lugged about as though they were unusually phlegmatic tabbies.

Despite the dire prophecies of neighbors, nothing untoward happened to the children; and as for the cats, they went the way of many a domestic Tom. They took to staying out all night, then to staying away for several days at a time; and, finally they did not come home at all. The last time my friend saw one of them he was up a telephone pole about a mile from the house and the other came out of the brush to the call, "Puss, puss."

Their current successor is an eleven-pound, five-month-old male of the same species who is even more completely a member of the family. He is housebroken and most of his behavior is precisely that of a domestic cat. He is very playful and, like many house cats, he walks about the edge of the bathtub while the children are being bathed, apparently fascinated by the human being's strange lack of distaste for water. When he makes a playful leap from five feet away to land on your chest or lap, the impact is considerable; but in many ways he is gentler than a kitten, or, perhaps one should say, seems more aware that his teeth and claws are potentially dangerous. Unlike most kittens, he makes "velvet paws" the inviolable rule and when he kicks with his hind legs in response to being tickled on the belly he keeps the murderous claws of his hind feet carefully sheathed—as a house cat usually does not.

I am not suggesting that always and for everybody a wildcat is a safer pet than *Felis domestica*. It may very well be that the adults are undependable; that they may, as is often said, be capable of sudden flashes of savagery; or, that at the best they are likely to have an inadequate idea of their strength and weight. But to play with so gentle a specimen of what is commonly thought one of the wildest of wild animals is to wonder just how much justification there is for loose talk about "natural ferocity."

What is the "true nature" of this beast? Or is the question as badly phrased as it is when you ask about the "true nature of man"? In both cases the only proper answer may be that both are capable of many different things and that to judge the potentialities of the wildcat by what he is like when truly wild is as misleading as it would be to judge the potentialities of man by studying only the behavior of an Australian bushman.

I have never agreed with those enthusiasts who maintain that a man is "nothing but" what his social environment has made him. But I most certainly do believe that such environment has a good deal to do with his behavior. And though the extent to which the same thing is true of animals is considerably less, the fact remains that you can't know what an animal is really like unless you have known him as different environments have influenced him.

Some scientists are very loth to accept any observations that pet owners have to offer. Not without justification they distrust in fond parents that overinterpretation which is almost as inevitable in the case of a beloved animal as it is in the case of a child. Either is always given the benefit of the doubt. Happy accidents are assumed to be the result of intelligent foresight and the dog lover is often as sure that he can understand the precise semantic significance of a bark as the fond parent of a first child is sure that "aaaa" means "I love Mama."

Despite all this it is still true that the honest observation of well-treated pets can provide data as scientifically valid as any other. What a wild animal is like in the wild can be learned only by observing him in that state; but what you learn is relevant to that state only. In a different environment he becomes something else as surely as a man, moved from one environment to another, changes somewhat as a result of the change.

For the study of anything other than the most mechanically invariable behavior patterns, a pet is certainly a far better subject than a mere laboratory animal. If the pet is, as it is some-

times objected, "under artificial conditions," at least these conditions are no more artificial than those of the laboratory and
are more likely than the laboratory to expand rather than to
freeze latent potentialities. In some ways a pet is more than a
wild animal; in a laboratory, any creature is less—as anyone who
has ever looked at such a captive with a seeing eye could not
have failed to observe. In their loveless imprisonment the more
intelligent seem to question and to brood over their Kafka-
esque doom. It has imprisoned them for a crime of which they
are unaware and prepared for them some future they cannot
imagine.

Many of even the animals not commonly made pets respond
gladly to the kindlier conditions life with human beings provides. Even in zoos—which are at best little better than model
prisons—they develop an awareness of and an interest in people of which we would never suppose them capable if we knew
them only in the wild. And it is not by any means merely an
interest in the food which human beings sometimes provide.
Monkeys are notorious exhibitionists and gibbons, especially,
will put on performances at intervals after a preliminary bal-
lyhoo of howls to collect an audience. Less spectacular performances by simpler animals are even more interesting—as, for
instance, that regularly indulged in by a group of small ground
squirrels in an animal collection with which I happen to be
familiar.

These creatures were born in the very glass case where they
now live. While still babies they learned to climb up one side
of the case, hang momentarily from the roof, and then drop
from it to the floor. As time went on they made less and less
contact with side or roof until presently they were turning back
somersaults with only a kick against the roof at the height of a
circle. This performance attracted much attention from the
spectators. Now, one need only take up a position in front of the
case to have one or more of the squirrels assume his stance and

make several rapid flip-overs. Would one ever have suspected from observing these creatures in the wild that they were capable of enjoying the admiration of human beings? Does vainglory find a place in such tiny bosoms? For how many millions of years has the desire to show off existed?

The most objective observer—if he does actually observe—cannot help being struck by the change that comes over an animal who has been really accepted as a companion. Not only cats and dogs but much less likely animals seem to undergo a transformation analogous to that of human beings who are introduced to a more intellectual, more cultivated, more polished society than that in which they grew up.

It is not merely that they adapt themselves to new ways. Their very minds seem to develop and they become more aware of other creatures, including man, as members of a society, not merely as potentially dangerous or useful objects. The human voice, especially, seems to fascinate and delight them. Except, just possibly, for monkeys and dogs, it is doubtful that they ever understand a word as such. The symbolic nature of language seems to be beyond them. But the emotion with which words are spoken communicates directly, and they seem capable of distinguishing many shades of it.

Beyond question it is true at least that they like to be talked to and that talking to them is very important if they are to be drawn into close association with human beings. As I know from experience, this fact is particularly if somewhat unexpectedly conspicuous in the case of geese, though it is much less so in that of ducks. A goose, like a dog, gets a different expression about the eyes if he is accustomed to having some human being speak to him. Thoreau describes the hen wandering about in the kitchen of an Irishman's shanty as "looking too humanized to roast well." "Humanized" is precisely the word, and it is astounding to what extent many animals can become, in that sense, humanized.

There are, of course, limits beyond which no animal can go and there is a great difference between what different species are capable of. The difference between the very slight extent to which my salamander was humanized and what a really intelligent ape is capable of is enormous. But in every case—and this is true of man also—there are limits. To each, nature seems to say: Thus far shalt thou go and no farther. But we never know just how far a man or a beast can go until he has been given a chance. In neither case do the underprivileged furnish a fair answer.

How true this is is well illustrated in the two recent books *King Solomon's Ring* and *Man Meets Dog* by the distinguished Austrian observer Konrad Lorenz. His orthodox training as a scientist warns him against those pitfalls of overinterpretation and anthropomorphism which behaviorists are so eager to expose. But instead of taking it for granted that animal behavior is always explicable in either mechanistic or anthropomorphic terms, he tries to discriminate and to recognize the genuine difference between behavior which is merely mechanically conditioned and that which seems to suggest in the animal rudimentary powers analogous to the human.

Not a man to fear the ridicule of neighbors, he has been observed quacking encouragingly as he crawled through tall grass followed by a line of baby ducks who seemed to take him for their mother. In this instance he was demonstrating not that the ducklings have any evident awareness of the situation, but that they are the victims of what seems to be a merely mechanical conditioning. Like some other animals they are born with a mechanism which is ready to click when they open their eyes. The first moving object they see becomes the thing they are determined to follow. If that first moving object is a man, they will follow him in preference to the mother duck whom they may have seen a few moments later. If, on the other hand, they see her first, it has already become very difficult if not impossible to teach them to follow anything else. This does not mean that all newly born animals have this curious mechanism. Many which have not do nevertheless also operate like a machine, though like a machine differently set up. To account for their behavior or for that of the baby duck it is not necessary to assume any psychic process distinguishable from the mere mechanism of the conditioned reflex.

But Mr. Lorenz does not stop there. He has lived intimately with mature specimens of much more intelligent fowl—especially the highly intelligent raven. Though some of its behavior may be as mechanical as that of the duckling, other actions seem less obviously so. Still others, especially those relating to its intimate association with man and its development of personality, seem to suggest not mechanism but a genuine psychic activity. And it is this which has led Lorenz to invent the new word he uses to describe errors of interpretation which are the opposite of those against which we have so often been warned. "Mechanomorphism," or the stubborn determination to see everything in terms of the machine, may be a fallacy as serious as anthropomorphism.

There are, to be sure, some psychologists who still insist that neither man nor any other animal ever exhibits any behavior not either instinctive or conditioned. To them the final triumph of what they continue to call by the Greek word meaning "the science of the soul" is to have demonstrated that nothing remotely resembling a soul, not even reason or the power of choice, really exists at all. But unless one accepts this thesis the most interesting as well as the least understood branch of psychology is that which does attempt to investigate those actions and those mental states which cannot be shown to be the result of mechanically operating laws.

What makes such studies as those pursued by Lorenz so exceptionally impressive is the fact that he not only recognizes the existence of such phenomena in animals as well as man but also the fact that association with human beings seems to liberate in animals their psychic freedom very much as, so it seems, civilization liberates them in man. Perhaps the chief difference between human and animal psychology, as between the psychology of the lower and the higher animals also, is simply that in both cases what "higher" really means is "exhibiting a more extended range of phenomena which cannot be accounted for in terms of mere 'conditioning.' "

Even more striking in certain respects are two recent English books, Len Howard's *Birds as Individuals,* which describes the surprising and often highly individual behavior of wild birds (especially titmice) who had been left their liberty but invited into the house, and *Sold for a Farthing* by Clare Kipps, which recounts the life story of a tame sparrow. Both these observers are amateurs, but Julian Huxley has vouched for both so far as their reports on the actual behavior of their companions is concerned, and he is ready to grant that they seem to have demonstrated that birds are capable of what might be called "social adjustment" to a degree not hitherto suspected.

What seems to have surprised both Huxley and other commentators even more than the adaptability and apparent intelligence of creatures generally assumed to be less intelligent than many mammals is the extent to which the birds also exhibited individual variation and differences of temperament; the extent, in other words, to which members of the same species seemed to develop what we might as well call "an individual personality." Thus the experience of Miss Howard and Miss Kipps seemed to contradict not only laboratory experiments but also what has been observed of birds in freedom because both suggest that bird behavior is nearly always typical; that individuality hardly exists.

The distinguished American ornithologist Roger Tory Peterson has this to say:

The point that Miss Howard emphasizes . . . is that birds are *individuals.* Their actions often seem to demonstrate some sort of bird intelligence and do not always fall into the oversimplified mechanical patterns which some of us have come to accept. . . . As Dr. Niko Tinbergen, the great behaviorist of Oxford University, comments in *Ibis,* "Miss Howard describes most amazing things, and critical zoologists and psychologists, if not familiar with the ways of birds in the wild, may tend to armchair incredulity. . . . I have no such doubts, however." No other bird book in years has been the subject of so much discussion in England as has Miss Howard's. Some critics may feel that she occasionally resorts to anthropomorphic expressions. . . . Others may differ with her interpretations, but these should in no way be confounded with her facts. Her observations are very careful and her descriptions sensitive and honest. It is a most unusual story she has to tell.

Should we dismiss the new evidence or should we say that the professional observers of wild birds have been wrong?

What puzzled commentators seemed to have overlooked is a third possibility. Perhaps Miss Howard's birds not only *seemed* to have more individuality than wild ones but actually did have it. And perhaps they had it simply because they had moved into a social situation where individuality was recognized and given an opportunity to develop. In Bernard Shaw's *Pygmalion* the flower girl who is taught how to pass herself off as a member of sophisticated society announces an important discovery which she has made, namely, that it is not the way you behave but *the way you are treated* which makes the difference between those who are "ladies" and those who are not. Is there any reason why the same should not be, to a lesser extent, true of birds? To reconcile observations made upon any wild animal in a wild environment with those on the same animal after it has become accustomed to treatment as a pet it is not necessary to assume that the original observations were in any way defective or incomplete. Perhaps the seeming conflict merely reveals the fact that animals have a potential capacity for both a degree of individuality and a comprehension of a situation which the circumstances of wild life do not provide an opportunity to develop.

Many modern theorists seem to me to overemphasize a good deal the extent to which men are what "nurture" rather than "nature" makes them. But perhaps in the case of animals we have rather underemphasized it. What it may all come down to is simply that animals, like men, are capable of being *civilized* and that a civilized man or a civilized animal reveals capacities and traits which one would never have suspected in the savage.

We are no longer as surprised as our grandfathers were that an African native who has gone to Oxford can become so typically an Oxford man. Neither by studying an African savage in his native state nor by taking him into a laboratory would we ever be led to suspect the potentialities which can make him an Oxford man. Why then should we find it hard to believe that an analogous change may occur when a wild animal is given an analogous opportunity?

A few years ago I had arranged to spend the night at one of the remote Hopi villages in the house of a young woman educated to be a teacher in a distant Indian school but accustomed to spend her vacations in her native town. When I insisted that for dinner I wanted only that standby of travelers not quite sure of a cuisine, namely ham and eggs, she protested: "After all that is two proteins."

In my instinctive arrogance I had to restrain an impulse to say, "Look here, no Hopi is going to prescribe my diet." But the situation was actually a very minor and superficial example of the phenomena which have compelled us to revise our whole conception of the nature of the difference between civilized and "primitive" minds. So far as difference in mental capacity is concerned it is now generally agreed that there is none—or that the primitives are if anything somewhat our superiors.

If you trust mental tests they seem to demonstrate that the average I.Q. of the Hopi Indian children is higher than that of the white. Most anthropologists seem to agree that there is absolutely no evidence that the human mind, as such, has improved at all during the last five hundred thousand years. All that civilization has done is to elicit potentialities. Hence there is no reason why a savage, taken young into a sophisticated environment, should not become, as he sometimes does, either very highly civilized or, for that matter, an aesthete and a decadent. Is there, then, any reason for doubting that Miss Howard's birds had become what no one who had observed them only in the wild would have supposed them capable of becoming?

That animals are less plastic than human beings is obvious, and so is the fact that the ultimate development they can reach in the direction of individuality is, absolutely, much more restricted. But their plasticity seems sufficient to make a civilized bird very different from a wild one. And that, of course, is the most striking aspect of the vertebrates' superiority over the superficially more advanced insect. The one has potentialities. The other is fixed and finished. Therefore we might put it this way: some of the limitations of the wild animal are, like those of the savage, merely cultural rather than inherent. Those of the insects are not.

Science recognizes as valid and important the distinction between wild animals and "domesticated" animals. The only other category which it admits, even parenthetically, is that which it labels "pets" and which it dismisses as hardly worthy of scientific consideration. What I am suggesting in all seriousness is that full recognition should be given to that other category which I call "civilized."

The pet may or may not fall within it, depending upon how it is treated. Many show animals, no matter how pampered they may be, are certainly not civilized and indeed hardly deserve even the name of pets. Many a mongrel dog or cat, as well as many another creature of some species only occasionally adopted into human companionship, is much more than a mere pet simply because it is treated with understanding and with love; because it is accepted if not exactly as an equal, at least with some understanding of the fact that it is capable of responding to a kind of attention and consideration which many kindly people never think of according to even a cherished pet.

The merely domesticated animal, in contrast, is not only something less than a civilized one but something radically different. It has ceased to live the life of nature without being given the opportunity to live any other. Its instincts have faded and its alert senses have sunk into somnolence. Much has been taken away and nothing has been given in return. Such a merely domesticated animal has become a sort of parasite without even developing those special adaptations that make the true parasite interesting in some repulsive way. It is merely parasitic by habit, not by constitution, and of all the animals it is the least rewarding to study because there is almost nothing which can be learned about it. The human analogue is the degenerate remnant of some primitive race which lives upon the fringe of a somewhat more advanced society but has become incapable of leading its own life without having learned any other. Natural history should, on the other hand, no more neglect the civilized animal than anthropology should neglect the civilized man. Without some consideration of both we cannot possibly know what either man or any other animal is capable of.

One of the most important, one of the most fateful developments of thought during the last few centuries has been that which stresses the closer and closer identity of human with animal nature. And that has meant, on the whole, not a greater respect for animal traits and powers and potentialities, but less and less respect for man's. Those potentialities which had once been assumed to be exclusively human now came to be regarded as less and less substantially real. Man was thought of as "nothing but" an animal and the animal was held to be incapable of exhibiting anything except what had formerly been thought of as "our lower nature."

If we are ever to regain a respect for ourselves it may be that we shall regain it by the discovery that the animals themselves exhibit, in rudimentary form, some of the very characteristics and capacities whose existence in ourselves we had come to doubt because we had convinced ourselves that they did not exist in the creatures we assumed to be our ancestors. Even if man is no more than an animal, the animal may be more than we once thought him.

No doubt there are those to whom the concept of the "civilized" animal will seem fantastic and the suggestion that man may regain his self-respect by learning to understand better his animal ancestors even more absurd. To call an animal civilized rather than merely domesticated is, so they will say, to imply that he is to some extent capable of sharing in what are purely human prerogatives. But such an objection is most likely to be raised by the more dogmatic evolutionists, who are, as a matter of fact, those who have the least right to assume a qualitative rather than a merely quantitative difference between the inherent capacities of man and the other animals.

Either man is unique or he isn't. If he is unique then he cannot possibly descend through an unbroken line from the lower animals. If he does descend, or ascend, through such an unbroken line then each of his capacities must have at least its embryonic analogue in the simpler creatures who preceded him.

Evolution implies development, not the sudden appearance of something totally new. No such totally new capacity could have evolved at all, but would have had to have come suddenly into being. And one of the most important of man's capacities is that which enables him to do more than simply "adapt himself to changed conditions." It is the capacity to develop those unsuspected potentialities that makes "civilized" mean something more than merely "adapted to group life in a technologically complex society." An essential part of that something more is the development of a more varied, more vivid psychic life. And this is precisely the something more which the civilized animal also unexpectedly manifests.

6.

The Anthropomorphic Cat

Frances and Richard Lockridge

When we tell the cat Gin she is "bad" because she catches birds, there are certain evidences she knows what we mean. Her ears may move back a little; she looks at us with what seems to be doubt in her slanting blue eyes. She does not go away, knowing that from us no physical violence will follow, but she does not come closer, rub against us purring, as she is likely to do when we say, "Nice Ginny. Good Ginny." One might suppose that the word "bad" had a special meaning for her, and even that it meant to her what, more or less, it does to us. Things far more improbable are supposed by many people about cats.

Actually, if we do not altogether imagine the change we think we see in Gin when she hears the word "bad," it is probable that she is reacting to a tone rather than to a word. Cats are responsive to the timbre of the human voice, as dogs are; if we called Gin a "bad cat" in the tones of affection we employ when we praise her, there can be no doubt she would come to us with her low-pitched remarks of pleasure and hold her head up to be

SOURCE: From the book *Cats and People* by Frances and Richard Lockridge. Copyright 1950 by Frances and Richard Lockridge. Reprinted by permission of the authors and their agents, James Brown Associates, Inc., and of J. B. Lippincott Co.

stroked. It is by no means true that Gin understands every word we say to her, or even appears to. There are several human words incomprehensible even to Martini, and she may be a cat genius and is certainly of superior mentality.

But if Gin, and even Martini, actually understood the word "bad," or any of its gradations or opposites, neither would understand the concept, which is human and not feline and which is applied to cats by people with a childlike naïveté which would, in itself, puzzle any cat. Almost no cat is naïve; if we had not learned through long experience to be wary of generalization about these friends of ours, we would say flatly that no cat is ever naïve. But that would mean only that we had never known a cat whose behavior reminded us of the behavior of a naïve human being. Many cats may seem naïve to other cats; the whole feline apparatus for revealing this, and other characteristics, may be quite different from the human apparatus. It is entirely possible that cats do not behave like human beings, and it is even possible that they have no desire to, although humans generally try to make them do so and almost always think of them as if they were rather peculiar and on the whole somewhat backward men and women.

This tendency to anthropomorphize the cat—to ascribe to it human characteristics and, as a logical result, to insist that it mimic human behavior in so far as it can—begins very early in the human mind and continues very late. Children think thus about the cat and so, as we presently shall see, did the late Dr. Edward Lee Thorndike, who was not in other respects notably childlike. It is an attitude of mind which is very convenient for the human, and one into which the human almost inevitably falls. Probably, indeed, it is unavoidable; probably the only tribute the human mind can pay to objectivity is a realization that it has not been attained. Even this tribute is rarely paid; there is, for example, every evidence that Dr. Thorndike not only sought scientific objectivity when he tested the intelligence of cats but believed he had found it, although almost nothing could have been further from the truth. In his whole approach to the feline mind, this very great psychologist behaved embarrassingly as did 2,835 children who, almost fifty years ago, were asked about their pets by G. Stanley Hall and C. E. Browne. The children thought of cats as small humans with fur and four legs; so, essentially, did Dr. Thorndike.

Most of the Hall-Browne children did not, as a matter of fact, write about cats at all, since 71.6 percent of them preferred dogs—a statistical indication of some interest and one of the few which science seems to have made available on the subject. Whether the ratio of preference continues into the human's later years is uncertain; probably it does to a considerable degree, although many people come to know and admire cats as they grow more mature and less in need of that assurance of superiority which the attention of a dog provides. Certainly at any age, at least in the United States, more people are dog than cat addicts and there is a social pressure to reveal that preference. This is particularly true of the male. It is "manly" to have a dog as a small boy—and it is also a great deal of fun, and dogs are durable in relation to small boys as cats seldom are. Of the 804 young cat fanciers queried by Dr. Hall and his associate, 582 were little girls and only 222 young males.

These 804, regardless of sex, liked the cat because of the way it played, were captivated by its grace in movement and the constancy of movement. (Most of the children probably knew kittens or young cats, and these are almost never quiet, except when, suddenly, almost without warning, they go sound asleep.) The movements of cats are infinitely varied; no cat does things precisely as another cat does, and few cats repeat their own movements, even when performing essentially identical actions. (Sherry, for example, has a peculiar twisting leap in play, going into the air to avoid the onslaughts of a bit of paper, turning in the air like an acrobat, as if pivoted on her right shoulder, coming down still facing the plaything with four feet planted and back a little arched. We have never seen another cat make precisely these movements, although we have seen many cats perform what is essentially the same play antic. And Sherry does not do her leap each time, or perhaps ever, with identical movements. There is nothing mechanical about it as there is, for example, about the forehand drive of a good tennis player.)

Almost without exception, the children who liked cats for these habits and accomplishments thought of the cats as if they too were children, ascribing to them the same motives, requiring of them adherence to the moral standards the children had been taught, usually—no doubt to the astonishment of the cats—feeding them the same food that children like to eat or are required to eat. Most of the children were certain their cats talked to them by purring, moving eyes and heads and tails in certain fashions, and were certain they knew what the cats were saying. The cats said, "I love you" to their young playmates; said, "I want some milk," "Open the door, please," "Don't be cross with me," "I'm sorry; I won't do it again." The cats also said, "I want my dinner," and were rewarded with some remarkable embellishments to the normal feline diet of raw meat.

The cats were fed ice cream, which most cats do like; they were also fed peanuts, candy and custard pie, all of which most children like better than most cats do. They also, in homes where the child's diet was carefully supervised, got milk and cream, eggs, cereals and meat. A few of them, the children reported, ate mice and rats and fish, but the child mind clung to the conviction that the cats really preferred peanuts and hard candy, since what child does not?

"The child's attitude toward the cat is largely anthropomorphic," Dr. Hall wrote in his conclusions, published in 1905 in the *Pedagogical Seminary*.

He attributes to the cat the same thoughts and feelings which he himself experiences and in his treatment of his pet unconsciously reveals his own standards of right and wrong, his tests of affection, his preferences and dislikes. In this connection one of the most interesting points brought out is the child's inclination to make the test of right and wrong an objective conformity to the will of the owner. . . .

Children have the old conception of animals as moral beings fully responsible for the moral or immoral quality of their acts. In very few instances were the natural instincts of the cat taken into account; though catching rats and mice is often accounted a virtue, the catching of birds is designated as badness. It may be that in this moral objectivity there is a reflection of the regime to which the child himself has been subjected, for it is unfortunately too common to find children who regard an accident to their clothing or to property on the same plane with a moral offense, because the same punishment is meted out to both.

Dr. Hall decided also, from the data before him, that from their cats children derived a sense of authority, based largely on their superior size and strength—always desiderata when moral standards are to be established and kept in force. The investigator was left with the further conviction that keeping pets helps children develop a sense of responsibility and a humane attitude toward animals—which might, conceivably, later be broadened into a humane attitude toward humanity.

From the child to the adult mind is only a little step; sometimes, one suspects, it is not even that. Growing up, one may discover that cats prefer ground beef to peanuts; one may never learn that cats and other animals are not beings with man's morality; that to them it is naïve and impertinent to apply such terms as "good" and "bad," charge such sins as cruelty. "Objective conformity to the will of the owner" may be asked and even insisted upon, although with a cat it is not at all likely to be achieved. But it cannot be characterized, cannot be called "good," unless we are willing to abandon all but the crudest standards of morality. It is obvious, of course, that in most of mankind's relations with other animals, to say nothing of his own inter-tribal relations, it is precisely these crude standards which are accepted. No doubt it is too much to hope that men will be more perceptive in their contacts with cats than they are in their contacts with other men.

But until men give over applying these human standards to cats there is little chance of establishing that confident understanding between the two orders of the mammalia which should be the goal of all men and all cats. There is no use expecting cats to behave like human beings, and in a good many areas of activity it is as well that they do not. It is, for example, no good hoping that cats will become humane and abandon practices which man, an authority on the subject, considers cruel.

It was cruel, and human, to behave as the jailers of the Inquisition are reported—no doubt libellously—to have behaved toward certain prisoners they would torment. Their unfortunate victims, long locked in darkness, hoping to see light again only in the flickering fires of the auto-da-fé, were sometimes given brief glimpses of miraculous hope. A cell door was not, perhaps, securely locked or, carelessly as it seems, an instrument was left available with which it could be opened. The prisoner, hope faintly stirring, would begin his escape and find that, true enough the door would open, that the corridor outside it was deserted.

Then would begin a long, toilsome creeping toward the light; a cautious movement through stone corridors, quick retreats into available niches, ascents of interminable flights of stairs. And always this flight from darkness would be aided, would seem to be aided, by many tiny miracles—by jailers who did not look when hiding was impossible and discovery would have been certain; by doors unaccountably left unlocked, chains insecurely stapled. So, with hope growing slowly, the prisoner crept toward the light—crept until finally, at the end of a dark corridor, he could finally see the light; could see it through an open door, could stumble forward, blinded by light, a little more rapidly. It was not until he was almost at the door, could feel the outer air on his face, that the men who had been waiting stepped from concealment and put chains again on the miscreant and, one supposes, laughed. It was very amusing, very human—and very cruel, this cat-and-mouse game.

It is, of course, not too unlike the game the cat plays with the mouse, although it is more ingenious in the torment it inflicts, since man is a more ingeniously sadistic animal than a cat. The only difference is that man knows better and the cat does not; that in doing such things man violates, derides, his own humanity. Man puts himself not on the level of the cat, but on an infinitely lower level, because the cat is cruel only by man's standards and not by his own. There are no humanitarian cats; none to say, as men have said when man's history was darkest, that certain things are unworthy of cats; no cat has ever formed the concept of "cruelty" and so, essentially, no cat can be cruel. When men do what cats do, men are cruel. They often do; one does not need to go back to the Inquisition to find proof of this in man's history. "Even owners of factories employing child labor and dramatic critics have told me that cats are cruel," Carl Van Vechten remarks quietly in his famous book on cats.

Many others, in more tenable moral positions, have made that charge and amplified it and always, as when they call the cat "sly" and "crafty," they have been anthropomorphizing the cat and, at the same time, sentimentalizing the cat. The two things go together; they are parallel manifestations of the difficulty men have always had in looking at the cat as a cat, and agreeing that it be allowed to remain a cat. Possibly man has been misled by his experience with dogs, because it is much easier to apply to dogs the standards to which humans verbally adhere and to get the dogs to play along.

It is easy, indeed, to believe that the dog would very much like to be a man, just as man would like to make himself over in the image of God. The ambition of a well-brought-up dog— that is to say, of a "good" dog—is to please his master before himself and the means he employs to accomplish this are commonly more human than subtle. He is demonstrative in displays of affection as many people are, and as almost all people would like others to be toward them; the dog leaves you no doubt where you stand and when he gives his devotion, as he does readily, he is apt to give it fulsomely, so that for a little while the meanest human can see himself godlike in the dog's beaming eyes. The dog is uncritical; one of the best known dogs of literature belonged to Bill Sikes, certainly one of literature's meanest men, and followed his master to death in, it must be admitted, one of the most improbable scenes of melodrama ever to come from human pen. Dogs are continually wasting away on the graves of their deceased masters, dying of broken hearts during less permanent separations and otherwise behaving with an almost human lack of reticence. If you want to go for a walk, there is nothing a good dog wants more; if you want to sit by the fire, so does the dog, looking up now and then from his sleep with tender eyes, making sure that you have not left him. If you want to play games, the dog will learn them eagerly, and play them with zest; a dog may be trained to walk on his hind feet, which makes him ridiculous, and to "speak" for his dinner. If he had the words, he would no doubt be happy to recite for company.

This canine desire to do everything the human wishes, to shape his whole life to human rather than to canine preferences, is naturally very gratifying to man. It supports man's assurance that he is in all respects superior, corroborates his belief that all animals would be simian if they could. And it makes the dog lovable to all people capable of affection; it is difficult to see how anyone can resist a dog, whose whole being is bent on proving himself irresistible. The dog is a sunny animal; if he had ever been a god, he would have been a god of light. And if, as Nelson Antrim Crawford has unkindly suggested, he now and then reminds one of a bond salesman, there is no harm in bond salesmen and they, also, tend to be creatures of the greatest cordiality.

It is also easy to understand a dog, at least superficially. One may assume, with some safety, that when a dog behaves as a human would under given circumstances he is feeling as nearly as he can as a human would under those circumstances. When a dog smiles, he smiles like a man. When he greets his master with bounds of delight, he clearly feels delight; he is a human throwing arms about a returned loved one. When a dog licks you, it is probable that he is kissing you. (When a cat licks you, it may well be to see how you taste.) A dog who is spoken to crossly sinks into shame and abasement, and does it noticeably; a whipped dog cowers as a whipped man does—or, if the man's pride will not let him, longs to do. To a kind word following punishment, the whole dog brightens. The authority one can exercise over a dog provides a gratification hardly to be equalled now that human slavery is, in some parts of the world, abolished.

And, because he is convinced that man knows best—is convinced, surely, that man *is* best—the dog will accept, or seem to accept, man's codes of behavior. Often, indeed, he accepts them much more wholeheartedly than man does. One can persuade a dog that it is "wrong" to eat canapés from the coffee table and it is reported to us by dog owners that many dogs will continue not to eat canapés even when humans are absent. We knew, for many years, a fox terrier who had been persuaded it was "wrong" to go to the second floor of the house he lived in and who consequently never went there, even when the family was away. (He was believed not to, at any rate, and since he was always shedding on the furniture he was reasonably easy to trace.) The same dog, who never seemed to us notable in intelligence, knew it was "wrong" to sleep on the downstairs furniture, but that temptation was more than he could resist. He always, however, got down when he heard the family coming, and always landed on the floor with a revealing thump. He retained for some minutes after these violations of the code the expression so aptly called "hang-dog."

No cat we have ever known would have got off the chair in deference to human wishes and there is no facial expression that can be called "hang-cat." Nor have we ever known a cat who considered it "wrong" to eat all the canapés he could reach, if he liked them, although we have taught one or two that it may prove inexpedient. A cat's interests remain feline, not human, as do his habits. If he likes you—and cats often fall in love with people—it is because he approves of you as an individual; he makes allowances for your humanity, but he does not envy it. All his ways are his, and none of them are human. It is clear that he would not be a human if he could.

This refusal to fit into an anthropomorphic pattern irritates many people, and particularly those who like to keep life simple and on a plane of ready understandability. It is difficult to understand a cat, who persists in being "different," a vice which many humans cannot tolerate, even in other humans.

7.

The Origins and Stages of Animal Domestication

F. E. Zeuner

Many theories have been put forward attempting to explain the domestication of animals by man. Nearly all of them have in common the basic conception of a purposeful procedure, that man needed a supply of certain animals and therefore contrived to domesticate the species in question. This applies to Hahn's (1896) theory of a religious origin—the animals being first domesticated for use as sacrifices—as well as that of Hilzheimer and others that domestication was invented to satisfy economic needs, like supply of meat and skins.

But in theories of this kind the difficulty is apt to be overlooked that Mesolithic man (for it was in the Mesolithic that domestication began) would have found it far easier and more economic to obtain the necessary supplies by hunting and trapping, just as his forefathers had done, instead of embarking upon experiments of taming unwilling animals that would reward him for his efforts only after several generations.

SOURCE: Frederick E. Zeuner, *A History of Domesticated Animals*, pp. 36–43, 46–49, 51–63 (excluding photos). Copyright © 1963 by Frederick E. Zeuner. Reprinted by permission of Harper & Row Publishers, Inc., and Hutchinson Publishing Group, Ltd.

THE BIOLOGICAL APPROACH

The fruitful approach to the problem of domestication is the biological one. The problem resolves itself into a simple and natural process if one adopts the practice advocated here of considering man as an integral part of his physico-biological environment. It is then found that the habits of man on the one hand and of certain animal species on the other made the appearance of domestication almost inevitable.

To understand this, it is necessary to remember that the social relation called "domestication" is by no means restricted to man and his animal subordinates. Man has applied the same practice to members of his own species, though in this case it is usually called slavery, unless a more euphemistic word is used.

Nor is man the only species of the animal kingdom which practises slavery or domestication. There are so many cases of the subjugation of one species by another that no more than a few examples can be given. These, however, must be regarded as truly relevant to the subject, for they clearly show, in my opinion, the way which in all probability man took when he had reached that crucial stage of his social evolution which led to the appearance of slavery in the widest sense.

Domestication presupposes a "social medium." As a rule the social evolution of a species must have reached a certain level before domestication becomes possible. This applies both to the domesticator and to the domesticated, though there are exceptions. In the case of domestication by man, the only notable exception is the cat. All other domesticated animals have in the wild state a social life of some kind, forming packs or herds.[1]

1. The pig is at a very primitive level, forming merely associations of in-

Animals which naturally entertain social relations with members of their own species are more ready to do the same with members of other species. Mixed herds of zebra, gnu and other antelopes are commonly seen in Africa. It is therefore not surprising that the vast majority of species domesticated by man belongs to the gregarious hoofed animals. Similarly, domestication of one animal species by another occurs almost exclusively among the social insects, especially the ants.

To discuss the conditions found in the animal kingdom is well worth while, but in order to throw some light on the origins of domestication in the human species it is advisable to clarify the complex conditions observed in nature, and to introduce certain terms of social relationship. The kinds of social relations observed are linked by many intermediate cases; in fact, clearcut divisions do not exist. Nevertheless, it is convenient to use some kind of classification.

SYMBIOSIS

All conditions of permanent living-together of two different species are called symbiosis, provided both partners derive advantages from it. Perfect symbioses, from which both partners benefit, without suffering in one respect or another, are rare. As an example of two non-social species which enter frequently into such relationship, the well-known hermit crab with its rider, the sea-anemone, may be recalled. The crab is supposed to derive protection from the tentacles of the anemone, whilst the latter obtains food morsels from the meals of the crab. The crab is careful not to lose the anemone and transplants it when it changes house and moves into a larger snail-shell. The ane-

---

dividuals which forage together. The dogs (wolves, etc.) hunt in packs, though they are quite capable of leading a solitary life. All other ancestors of domesticated animals live in herds, often with a leader.

mone, however, is decidedly a passive partner and may, if one likes, be regarded as subject to the crab, and its position classified as one of slavery. This illustrates the rule that in a symbiosis the partners are rarely equal. . . .

Many more are known of unequal partnership which, however, is not sufficiently unequal to be called social parasitism. *Myrmica canadensis,* for instance, is an ant of northern North America, whose nest is occasionally found to be intertwined with that of a smaller ant, *Leptothorax emersoni.* This species can enter the galleries of the large one through minute openings, but not *vice versa.* Far from being hostile to their little neighbours, says Haskins (1945), the *Myrmica* welcome the *Leptothorax* with a sort of tolerant indifference, treating them much as dogs are treated by people who do not like dogs. But the *Leptothorax* lick the *Myrmica* and beg food from them, and are indeed willingly supplied with regurgitated drops of food juice. It cannot be said that the invaded colony suffers from the invasions of the little neighbours, though it is doubtful whether they derive advantage from them. Nevertheless, the behaviour of the *Leptothorax* almost makes them social parasites. While the going is good they live entirely by begging, though when the need arises they are capable of fending for themselves.

This case is instructive from the human point of view, for it is one of supporting another form of life, that is intrusive but is not an open enemy. There are men who feed the sparrows that have intruded into their domain, and there may well have been a stage of throwing morsels to wild dogs which invaded the camps of pre-Neolithic man, long prior to any realization of the possible economic use of dogs. Such acts are elementary manifestations of the solidarity of life, especially of related life. It is characteristic of most higher animals that have developed a social medium of some sort and which are not enemies. It finds a simple expression in animal friendships as they occur under conditions of domestication between cats and dogs, or, stranger still, between cats and tame birds. It finds a higher expression in man's desire to keep all sorts of pets, and its highest expression in the naturalist who finds supreme satisfaction in observing, understanding and feeling as one with other living creatures.

The tendency to suffer the presence of other species as pets perhaps appeared very early. Even Upper Palaeolithic man may have done this, though the form of his economy prevented him from developing this relationship to full domestication. There are tribes of Australian aborigines who illustrate this stage of pet-keeping. Except for the dog, they have never domesticated animals, but keep them as pets. Wallabies and opossums, bandicoots and rats, even frogs and young birds, are tied up in the camp, but they are not properly fed or cared for, and most of them soon die. Wallabies and opossums, and occasionally cassowaries, however, learn to fend for themselves in the camp area. It is noteworthy that the dingo is treated in the same fashion, tied up when young and released when he has got used to the human environment. Similarly, pets are kept by certain American Indians.

It cannot surprise us, therefore, that several authorities believe that the habit of keeping young animals as pets is at the root of domestication in general. In this form it is certainly an over-statement, but it is conceivable, and even probable, that pet-keeping provided one of the bases on which domestication on an economic scale developed later on. The mothering instinct of the human female may well have played a part in this process, too.

Pet-keeping is particularly likely to have played a part in the domestication of the dog. The scavenging habits of wild dogs brought them into contact with the human social medium, and the pups may occasionally have been adopted. It is very interesting to find that one of the camp-fire stories of the Africans of Calabar in southern Nigeria explains the origin of the domesticated dog exactly in this way.

According to this story, related by Yoti Lane (1946), a boy adopted a wild dog's pup, grew fond of it and brought it up in the village in spite of the attempts of the pup's mother to rescue her child. When fully grown, the dog induced a bitch to join him, and their litter became used to camp conditons immediately. They went out on hunting expeditions with their human friends. Subsequently the inhabitants of other villages imitated the practice.

It is of course not assumed that this folktale is a piece of surviving tradition, but it describes the way in which, in the views of a people who are still in close contact with their natural environment, the domestication of the dog might have come about.

Another theory which supposes that domestication came about under conditions of amicable relations assumes that totem animals, which are not killed by certain groups of humans, would become tame in the area in question. There is, however, a great difference between the taming of a totem animal (in any case an unusual event) and its economic exploitation under conditions of complete domestication. Moreover, animals which are now domesticated do not appear to be chosen as totem animals. Though totemism is perhaps as old as the Upper Palaeolithic, as witnessed by the bison-hunter of Lascaux, it is very improbable that it ever led to domestication.

The various examples of symbiosis here discussed are admittedly not all voluntary. A certain amount of coercion, i.e., transplantation into the social medium of the more intelligent species, or expansion of the latter into the social medium of the weaker species, is common. Yet it cannot be denied that both parties derive advantages from the condition; the animal living with man, in particular, finding personal safety and an easier and more ample food supply.

Food supply appears to have played a particularly important

part in the establishment of close association between animals and man. This is most obvious in the case of the scavengers.

SCAVENGING

Some species enter into a relationship in which one lives regularly on the food debris or other waste products of the other species. If the removal of the waste products is an advantage to the producer, scavenging might approach closely a true symbiosis. But scavengers often have the habit of preying on the host, especially on its progeny, as and when opportunity arises. Scavenging thus grades into social parasitism.

Many scavengers are, moreover, not closely bound to the host species. The jackal, for instance, can live perfectly well without man, but where human settlements are available he will enter into a loose and impermanent though nevertheless quite regular relationship with man, in which the mutual advantage is obvious enough. Though in other associations of the scavenging type the relations are permanent, the comparatively loose ones of the wild dogs are of great interest since they illustrate one of the ways in which domestication is likely to have begun.

Two social media, those of the wild dog and of man, overlap because man produces offal which the dogs will eat. There is no cause for enmity in this, unless one of the species interferes with the habits of the other or causes danger to life. This is in fact so in the case of hyaenas, for instance, which are prone to steal man's food reserves and are of too fierce a disposition for the establishment of friendly relations. They are not sufficiently sociable. The smaller species of wild dogs are in a different category. Not only are they afraid of man; their habit of associating in packs with a recognized leader affords the possibility of the transfer of allegiance to man, once he is recognized as a being of superior strength and cunning. The origin of the domesticated dog will be discussed later. In the present context our interest is focused on scavenging as a possible basis for the development of actual domestication. It is, however, obvious enough that not every scavenger is a prospective candidate for domestication. The requirements of non-interference and of mental disposition have been mentioned already. In these respects all existing wild dogs are not equally suitable. Jackals head the list in so far as they are unlikely to attack man. But their social level is lower than that of dogs that practise active hunting and for this reason would be more ready to form with man groups which, from their point of view, must be regarded as mixed packs.

The smaller races of wolves found in southern countries do a fair amount of scavenging as well as hunting. They would, therefore, appear to be the most amenable to domestication, but they also tend to regard human settlements as legitimate hunting grounds, from which they frequently steal goats, domestic dogs and even children, as for instance in India today. These propensities are most strongly developed in the large northern races of wolves, which, therefore, are the least likely to have provided the initial stock from which the domesticated dog emerged.

The combination of scavenging and robbing is of course exceedingly common in nature, and it has often provided the conditions for the evolution of regular pests and even parasites. Thus, whilst scavenging in its pure form is an example of symbiosis, it grades imperceptibly into exploitation of the host species by the scavenger. On the other hand, where conditions are favourable to domestication, it is evident that the scavenging species will in due course be exploited by the host.

The pig is another scavenger which has been domesticated. Since it occupies a low level on the social scale, its relations have rarely developed beyond those of an exploited captive.

Scavenging exhibits more clearly than any other social relationship the possibilities of further developments, either in the direction of pests and parasites (the guest exploiting the hosts) or in the direction of domestication (the hosts exploiting the guests).

The invention of agriculture brought in its train fresh opportunities for the development of guest-host relations, as the fields were liable to be regarded as excellent feeding grounds by several herbivorous and gregarious animals. So long as the fields lay fallow this condition would not be radically different from other cases of scavenging, but while the crop was growing the same practice of the animals constituted an act of robbery. Nevertheless, it did afford social contacts which in all probability led to the domestication of the aurochs and related large bovines, and perhaps other species also. . . .

DOMESTICATION OF THE REINDEER AS A CASE OF SOCIAL PARASITISM

There appears to be one example of domestication of an animal by man which may be regarded as falling into the category of social parasitism. It is that of the domestication of the reindeer.

For several reasons the reindeer represents a particularly interesting example of domestication by man. Both the domesticators and the domesticated have remained in the state of nomadism.[2] Nevertheless, the activities of man in relation to the reindeer can only be described as those of a social parasite. Like so many guests of ants and termites, the human species has even supplied a delicacy which the host species is eager to obtain. In so far, however, as the exploiting species gains the upper hand in this process and the exploited species degener-

2. Late developments are irrelevant in this context.

ates, the case of reindeer and man might equally well be discussed under the head of "true domestication," but since it appears to have begun as ordinary social parasitism it is more usefully treated at this point.

Of the several theories concerning the domestication of the reindeer, that which attributes its beginnings to the practice of decoy-hunting is the best-founded. This view was developed independently by Hatt (1919), the Danish anthropologist, and Sirelius (1916), the Finnish archaeologist. Hatt collected numerous records of reindeer-hunting by means of decoy animals and has reported on them with care. Only three variants of these may be quoted to illustrate the method. According to Pallas, the eighteenth-century traveller, the Samoyed hunt reindeer in the following manner: The hunter selects four or five tame reindeer, usually from the hinds and fawns. Holding them on ropes he approaches the herd of wild reindeer under their cover and against the wind, until he is near enough to shoot his arrow.

Another method is practised by the Tungus. It consists of leaving, during the rutting season, a few tame hinds on a feeding ground of the wild deer. The wild stags will associate with the hinds and are killed when the hunter returns after a day or two and approaches the group cautiously. Both the Tungus and the Samoyed employ strong tame stags during the rutting season. Ropes or thongs are tied round their antlers and they are sent off when a wild herd with a stag is in sight. The tame stag begins a fight with the wild one and the latter's antlers become entangled. He is held in this condition until the hunter arrives.

Tame deer which had proved their worth would naturally be protected and looked after by the hunter. Since tame hinds would mate with wild stags, fawns would be born in due course, and any hunter owning some decoy reindeer would almost unintentionally become a reindeer-breeder. The ease with which domestication of reindeer could be effected is largely due to the fact that the social state of man and of deer was the same, namely nomadism, and that neither was compelled to adopt any profound change of habits. Thus, to the present day the reindeer, both wild and domesticated, have remained a nomadic species, and so has man who follows the herds, preying on the wild and controlling and exploiting the tame.

In doing so he takes his toll of the species in much the same way as wolves do, and the only advantage that accrues to the domesticated reindeer is a very limited amount of protection from these and other predators. From the biological point of view this is a doubtful advantage, since the reindeer as a community have to pay heavily in individuals which, instead of being devoured by wolves and bears, are killed by man. The fact that man has adapted himself to the habits of the reindeer, as well as his numerical inferiority, make him a social parasite of the deer. The hunting of wild reindeer was not ended as a result of domestication. The more elaborate forms of exploitation of the domesticated deer, like use as a draught-animal, for riding, and as a milk-supplier, are of comparatively recent date, and evidently influenced by familiarity with cattle and horse.

At the onset of the process of domestication, man appears to have taken advantage of the greediness with which reindeer lick up salty matter. Human urine is regarded by them as the greatest delicacy, and it is this substance which attracts and binds reindeer to human camps. This craving is probably due to the lack of salt in the water available to reindeer, which is mainly derived from melting snow, though all ruminants are attracted by salt-licks. The reindeer nomads of course take full advantage of it, even today, so that the supply of a delicacy provides the meeting ground on which the social media of the two species "overlap." . . .

It should further be noted that deer are easily tamed when young and that it is not difficult to obtain fawns of any species. As young red deer were tamed as decoys in Germany until the Middle Ages, it is evident that the method of transforming fawns into decoys has been practised in widely distant areas. Nor is decoy-hunting with the aid of tamed young animals restricted to deer. Apart from birds, with which we are not concerned here but which have given the name to the method, both aurochs and bison appear to have been hunted in this manner. Reinhardt relates the ancient Frankish, Alamannic and Langobardian laws on decoy-hunting. The practice was common with red deer, but aurochs and bison were tamed also. Hatt rightly emphasizes the potential significance of this fact as follows:

May we suppose that the use of tamed oxen as decoys in the hunt was a feature characteristic of the initial stages of the domestication of oxen, although it persisted until the Middle Ages? In that case, the hunter's culture has been of greater importance to the early development of the domestication of animals, than has been supposed by leading philosophers.

Though this possibility has to be taken seriously, some difficulties arise when the decoy method is regarded as the only way in which the aurochs was transferred into the state of domestication. It is one proposition to tame specimens and to train them for special tasks. The circus director succeeds in doing so today with the most unusual kinds of animals. But to cause them to breed freely in captivity, and to make them forget their personal freedom, so that they stay with man without cage, fence or chain, is a very different matter. We shall have to return to this point shortly.

Other domesticated species which may have gone the way of the reindeer, and subsequently been compelled even to renounce their migratory habits, are the sheep, the goat and the horse. This is put forward as a suggestion. In the case of sheep and goat it is based on their natural habits; they are shy and fond of mountainous country and far less likely to invade fields than, for instance, pig or wild cattle. As to the horse, a pronouncedly nomadic species, it is likely to have been domesticated by nomadic peoples. . . .

TRUE PARASITISM

In insect societies social parasitism has repeatedly developed into true parasitism, the guest living exclusively on the body fluids of the host. Since there is hardly any parallel to this among mixed societies of the man-animal group, there is no need to go into details. The only case which could be placed in this category is that of the Masai, cattle-breeding nomads of East Africa who drink the blood of their cattle without killing them. An arrow is shot at close range into a vein in the neck, and the wound is closed with a plug after a certain quantity of blood has been obtained.

It is impossible to sort the various possibilities of social relationships between different species into hard and fast categories, and the classification adopted here is arbitrary in several respects. On the whole the examples so far discussed belong to cases in which the host species remains in control of the environment. Nevertheless, the balance occasionally shifts so much to the advantage of the guest (man-reindeer, *Lomechusa*) that the host is ruined by the guest. True domestication seems to have arisen more than once in this manner.

TAMING

There are many other cases in which a guest-host relation does not exist in the strict sense of the term, but where one species, whose social medium overlaps that of another, proceeds to limit the freedom of movement of the latter. This is, of course, a conspicuous feature in many cases of domestication by man. The meeting ground of the social media of two species is a purely geographical one, as they both inhabit the same area. The absence of the guest-host relationship presupposes systematic subjugation of one species by the other and compulsory incorporation in the social medium of the domesticator. One would expect this condition to be characteristic of man, which indeed it is, but it is not exclusive to man as it is very common among social insects. In both types of animal (i.e., in man and the social insects), however, this condition is not primitive and it appears only in the most highly developed social groups.

It is convenient first to give a few examples from the social insects. The ants of the genus *Polyergus* are keepers of slaves and their entire economy is adjusted to the presence of slaves in their colonies, hence slave-making is a necessity. The species *P. rufescens,* for instance, raids the nests of *Formica fusca* and other species of this genus. According to Haskins, the raids are carried out with great precision and brilliance. A powerful excitement pervades the raiding army which takes advantage of the moment of surprise when it attacks a *Formica* nest. Resisting *Formica* workers are killed and the young, especially the pupae, are carried away to the raiders' nest with great celerity. On arrival home the victims of the raid are handed over to the slaves already present who bring them up to become faithful servants of the colony. *Polyergus* has become so dependent on its slaves that all the domestic life of the mixed colony is conducted by the slaves, even the building of the nest. The slave-keepers themselves have restricted their activities to conducting wars and to loitering.

Many other varieties of slavery among social insects could be quoted. It will be noticed that the closest parallels exist between these examples among insects and cases of human slavery. We are not here concerned with these intra-specific examples, however. The inter-specific cases, in which man tames or enslaves another animal species, are those which fall under the heading of domestication.

Just as the ant communities of the *Polyergus* type have passed through stages of more primitive conditions of slave-keeping, it is more than likely that the taming of animal species which would not voluntarily enter into a guest-host relationship with man can only have occurred after man had already gathered experience in the keeping of domesticated animals. Such cases, therefore, are to be regarded as of a higher level of domestication. The guest-host relationships discussed earlier represent a more primitive and possibly more ancient condition. Once man was familiar with the practice of keeping animals like the dog or sheep, he might have conceived the idea of trying to keep other species which he was in the habit of hunting.

It is extremely difficult to visualize this happening prior to the beginnings of agriculture, because the initial social contact between man and the animal in question can only have been an unfriendly one. For example, elephants are utilized as slaves of man on the *Polyergus* principle. Sociologically independent ("wild") specimens are caught and compelled to work for man. The process of taming is much helped by the presence of previously tamed elephants, a remarkable parallel to the conditions under which *Formica* slaves enter into the social medium of the *Polyergus*. Nevertheless, the domestication of elephants has usually not proceeded beyond the stage of taming, for they are mostly allowed to breed in freedom and only captured from time to time. The reason for this is undoubtedly the large size of the animal.

It is very probable that the domestication of the large bovines also proceeded along similar lines. This is, of course, not meant to imply that bovines were originally caught in order to perform definite jobs for man, as is the case with the elephants today. But the first contacts of settled communities with large bovines which might have made them think of the possibilities of domestication, with which they were already familiar from the dog, goat and sheep, may well have been established by herds of wild animals robbing the fields, a habit of wild bovines today as much as of elephants. Attempts to tame young individuals of the bovine species may have been made at an early date in the Neolithic.

For some time a condition intermediate between taming and true domestication is likely to have existed, in which the tamed animals were allowed to interbreed with their wild relations. This practice is known to exist among certain reindeer-breeders, and among bovines it is illustrated by the mithan of Assam, already mentioned. The mithan are allowed to interbreed regularly with wild gaur, and this is considered a necessity in order to maintain the qualities of the domesticated stock. A serious obstacle to the incorporation of any large animal species within the social medium of man is the greater or lesser fierceness and intractability of its individuals. In this respect, however, man derives, quite "unintentionally," considerable advantage from keeping animals under unfavourable conditions.

The conceptions of stock-breeding which early Neolithic man may have had are not likely to have been of an advanced kind. In fact, his sole interest was to keep the animals subjugated, to make them docile and to use them to his own advantage. To give them the best possible living conditions and to provide them with the most suitable food were ideas not likely to have entered the minds of a race of men who were modest in regard to their own requirements of feeding and housing. Inevitably, therefore, animals kept in captivity must have deteriorated. Their progeny would have been smaller and weaker than their wild ancestors, and hence presumably more docile. I am inclined to think that the outcome of this process was the development of the so-called *Bos longifrons* type of cattle. Cattle of small size and great docility, in fact, must have been essential under early Neolithic conditions, and man obtained such cattle quite unintentionally by keeping them in, or near, his settlements.

Once the domestication of the species had been thoroughly

effected, however, the idea of increasing the body size is likely to have been regarded as useful, in order either to increase the meat supply or the working strength of the animals. Since under primitive conditions interbreeding with wild individuals was an easy matter, it is conceivable that this would at times have been regarded with favour by the breeders of the age. It is with the intention of improving the domesticated stock that the mithan and reindeer are allowed to interbreed with wild individuals today.

With increasing experience in the keeping of domesticated stock, it would also have occurred to prehistoric man from time to time to restart the entire process from fresh wild stock, which process, as well as that of allowing cattle to interbreed with wild individuals, is likely to have played a decisive part in the appearance of some of the so-called *primigenius* breeds of domesticated cattle.

SYSTEMATIC DOMESTICATION

It was only after man had gained considerable experience in the keeping of animals that he became capable of deliberately domesticating animals within short periods of time. It appears, however, that the majority of animals which are important from the economic point of view had been domesticated under conditions of scavenging, social parasitism and the like, before planned domestication was first undertaken. By that time the domesticated animals had proved their worth and played their part in the economic revolution of the Neolithic, and there was, therefore, little cause left to domesticate other species which would be no better than those already subjugated.

Nevertheless, it appears that many such experiments were made in Egypt in Old Kingdom times. Pictorial representations, such as those in the grave of Mereruka at Sakkhara, show

animals like gazelles, ibex, addax antelopes with collars round
their necks, not to mention monkeys and even carnivores like
hyaenas. Hyaenas in particular appear to have been kept and
stuffed like geese to make them fat. Many attempts were made
by civilized man to tame or, by allowing them to propagate
themselves in captivity, fully to domesticate animals. But most
were given up sooner or later, other than experiments with the
well-known standard stock of domesticated beasts.

There is only one species regarding which it is difficult to
construct a case of overlap of social media leading to domestication, and which does not fall into the category of crop-robbers
already mentioned. This is the domestic fowl, and it may therefore be suspected of having been domesticated by peoples who
were already familiar with the possibilities of domestication.
The fowl may originally have attracted man by its fighting habits and not so much as an economic proposition. Jungle fowl are
shy birds and would hardly associate themselves voluntarily
with man.

ANIMALS DOMESTICATED BY MAN

At this point it is advisable to refer briefly to the more important species that man has succeeded in domesticating. Broadly
speaking, and in accordance with a practice prevalent also
among social insects, it is likely that the individuals on which
domestication was tried were nearly always immature. Youngsters are less fierce than adults and adapt themselves more
readily to changed conditions.

It has been repeatedly emphasized in these pages that the
groupings made are inevitably arbitrary and that it depends
greatly on point of view to which category one is apt to assign
a species. This must be borne in mind in connection with the

following attempt to classify domesticated animals according to their social relationship to man.

There is a group of categories of early date, comprising scavengers and social parasites, which is likely to have arisen under very primitive conditions. This group does not necessitate agricultural activities and everything points to the cases in question having arisen while man was a nomad. The category of scavengers comprises the dog, the pig and the duck. That of social parasitism contains the reindeer, the sheep and the goat. Since many human communities have continued a nomadic life up to the present day, the time when domestication occurred need not always be particularly remote. But it is in these two categories that pre-Neolithic domestication is likely to be found. For the dog this has been established as a fact, for sheep and goat it is highly probable.

A later group comprises the categories of crop-robbers, the systematically domesticated and the pest-destroyers. These categories cannot be earlier than the beginnings of agriculture. The crop-robbers comprise cattle, buffalo, elephant, rabbit and goose. In the systematically domesticated category come fowl, hyaena, ostrich and recent acquisitions like domestic mouse, rat and canary. Thirdly, among the pest-destroyers which invade the social medium of man in pursuit of a prey that happens to be a pest, the cat, the ferret and the mongoose are prominent species.

Finally, one more group appears to exist which is of considerable historical interest. These are the animals domesticated by secondary nomads. Secondary nomadism occurs in regions where agriculture is no longer profitable because of deterioration of the soil. These nomads needed transport, and they domesticated the horse and the camel.

In the following paragraphs this classification will be discussed in some detail.

THE PROCESS OF DOMESTICATION

It is possible to generalize to some extent the process of domestication. In any particular instance there must have been an initial stage when our animal species had but loose ties with the social medium of man. Interbreeding with the wild forms must still have been common and kept the species close to the wild ancestor from the morphological point of view.

The second stage was one of completing the process of domestication, that is of subjugating large numbers of the species and of making these individuals wholly dependent on the social medium of man. This period was one of comparatively strict captivity, during which the domesticated beasts cannot have had much opportunity of interbreeding with their wild relations. The outcome of this process was a stock with distinct characters of domestication, such as different colour, reduction of body size and horns (if any) or the appearance of a frontal eminence in the *brachyceros* breeds of cattle, a reduction of the chewing apparatus in dogs and cats, and many other features. It was with domesticated stock which had successfully weathered the second stage that Neolithic man settled in Europe. He came with small and distinctive breeds of sheep, cattle and pig. Similarly, it appears that in Mesolithic times the domesticated dog came into Europe as a ready-made breed.

The third stage is marked by the beginning of intentional development of certain characters in the stock. There was an economic consideration in the size of domesticated animals as it was advisable to have large animals where these could be maintained, provided that they did not revert to the fierceness of their wild ancestors. For this reason one may suspect that Neolithic and Bronze Age man from time to time allowed interbreeding of the domesticated stock with wild animals. This applies to cattle in the first instance, but it appears that it also provided a means of developing more aggressive breeds of dogs from Maglemose times onwards.

This third stage passes imperceptibly into a fourth stage when man, the breeder, began to pay increasing attention to the qualities of the beast, both economic (milk and meat production, wool and so on) and morphological (horn shapes, drooping ears, colour and so forth). In the Middle East this fourth stage had been entered long before 3000 B.C., a time when very well-marked breeds of sheep, goat and cattle were already in existence.

During the fourth stage the domesticated stock was becoming standardized, and so different from the wild ancestral species that interbreeding with the wild must have been highly undesirable, for interbreeding would have spoilt the qualities which had been obtained laboriously through selection.[3] For this reason the wild species is likely to have come to be regarded as an enemy and this fifth stage, therefore, spells the doom of the wild ancestor. In fact, when a specialized stock, suiting man's purposes and well adapted to his social medium, was available, the inroads of wild relations into the domain of man would have been regarded as a serious nuisance. Since the domesticated beasts would supply all the economic needs the species in question could satisfy, except purely for sport, the wild relations were no longer wanted even for hunting. There are many medieval reports of the extermination of wild cattle, and the tarpan, the wild horse of south-east Europe, was exterminated by the local peasants partly because the tame mares were apt to elope with wild stallions.

As the wild species became rarer, the absorption of its last

3. A firm belief in the causal connection of characteristics helped in this process. Hair colour or horn shape and milk production, for instance, may have been believed to be linked, with or without reason. In any case, such views speeded up the standardization of breeds considerably.

remnants into the domesticated stock is bound to have happened frequently. It is known, for instance, that the last wild horses in the great game park of Count Zamoyski, situated at Zwierzyniec, near Bilgoraj, Poland, were caught and given to the peasants in 1812. Similarly, the Przewalskii horse of Mongolia has by now been almost completely absorbed into the domesticated stock of the nomads of the country. At an earlier date, this must have happened to the dromedary of Arabia. The process of extermination of the wild form has, however, everywhere been much accelerated by the destruction of its natural environment, either by deforestation or the spreading of plots of cultivation.

PROBABLE DATE OF THE EARLIEST DOMESTICATION

It is widely held that the domestication of animals is closely linked with agriculture, so much so that the development of animal husbandry without crop-raising is by some regarded as impossible. This view is in part based on evidence from excavations which show that animal husbandry and agriculture occur together, even in early Neolithic sites. There is, however, a psychological element present, namely a reaction to the earlier hypothesis that nomadic herding of animals preceded the agricultural stage, a hypothesis for which archaeological evidence had been scarce or missing. Before discarding it, however, it must be remembered that it may have a considerable element of truth.

First of all, the dog is an obvious and undoubted exception. From it one learns that, even under the less settled conditions of Mesolithic food-gathering, a symbiotic association of some animals with man might well have developed by way of scavenging, social parasitism or in some other way. In the case of the dog, evidence from prehistoric sites has actually been found, and it is fortunate that the dog remains from the Ma-glemose and other Mesolithic sites were recognizably domes-ticated. We owe a debt of gratitude to the dog species for devel-oping domestication characters so rapidly. Had this not been the case, and it is probable that other species responded more slowly, we should hardly have hesitated to regard the speci-mens in question as coming from races of wild wolves, and might even have construed a theory that these species were hunted.

Considering further the information provided by modern reindeer nomadism, it is evident that at the Mesolithic stage it would have been quite possible for man to attach himself to certain social ruminants, in the same manner as the Lapps and the Siberian reindeer nomads have attached themselves to that species. The only evidence which might be produced in support of such a view would be the concentration of the bones of the species in question in Mesolithic food refuse. In this respect, however, the evidence does not suggest the domestication of any species other than the dog. Nor could it be conclusive if such were found, since specialized hunting would produce a similar effect.

One comes, therefore, to the point of admitting that (quite apart from the dog) a social relationship, which may be de-scribed as a primitive condition of domestication, is at least conceivable in the Mesolithic. The species to which this would have been applicable would have been nomads themselves, or one should perhaps rather say seasonal migrants. There are several modern domesticated species which may be regarded as possible candidates for pre-Neolithic domestication, namely reindeer, goat, sheep, horse and camel. Of these, sheep and goat are known from the Belt Cave in Persia to have been domesticated since the earliest Neolithic, and the goat at Jeri-cho since 6710 B.C. at least. The initial stages of their domestica-tion may well lie much further back in prehistory, i.e., in the

Mesolithic. Moreover, the scarcity of evidence for nomadic animal husbandry, which at present is taken too seriously, is perhaps no more than a result of the scarcity of prehistoric nomads' sites, especially in those areas of western Asia where the domestication of several of our important animal slaves is likely to have begun.

In fact, the simple conditions of reindeer domestication, which are believed to have arisen by way of decoy-hunting, do not even exclude the possibility that the very first step towards domestication may actually have been taken in Upper Palaeolithic times. The first steps are bound to have been slow and made at considerable intervals. The suggestion that the reindeer-hunting economy of the Magdalenian and related cultures was perhaps supported by some primitive domestication has occasionally been timidly put forward. It has always been emphatically rejected. But we should be clear in our minds that the absence of evidence does not mean that the idea is wrong. Whilst hunting was still the dominant practice, it was after all not above the mental level of Upper Palaeolithic man, as we know him from other activities, to keep reindeer as decoy animals. It is really a small step from stalking in the disguise of a deer, whose horns and skin are worn by the hunter himself, to approaching the quarry hidden behind some live animals. But whilst I am not prepared to regard it as probable that Magdalenian man had already taken the first step towards domestication by keeping decoy animals, I do consider the question as sufficiently serious to deserve attention in the hope of finding some definite evidence either for or against. Even Lower Palaeolithic evidence for man's assumption of a "personal" relation to animals is not lacking.

There is one factor which, viewed in the light of the biological approach here advocated, supports the hypothesis of pre-agricultural domestication of ruminants. It is the sheepdog's performance. Evidently, if the dog joined man in the Mesolithic at the latest, why should it not retain its habits and continue to drive animals as wolves are wont to do? [An accompanying photograph, not reproduced in this edition, shows a wolf driving reindeer.] A tamed wolf would do the same. I therefore suggest that the comradeship between man and wolf led to a driving of certain nomadic animals, especially sheep and goats, and that Mesolithic man had already joined in this operation. The domestication of sheep and goats would thus have begun while the Mesolithic was still in full swing.

It must be admitted, then, that agriculture is not a prerequisite of domestication as such, and the domestication of certain species may well date far back into pre-Neolithic times. On the other hand, there are species which, for biological reasons, are not likely to have come into the orbit of man before agricultural operations had begun. Chief amongst these are cattle. Furthermore, the Neolithic revolution was a change that placed an enormous economic premium on the art of animal domestication, which in consequence became established as a universal practice. On the other hand, the advanced state of domestication, in which movements of animals were completely controlled by man, was clearly impossible in pre-Neolithic times. So long as man was moving with the animals he might have been able to develop domestication to the level exemplified by the reindeer today. But to proceed to the stage of confining animals to restricted spaces man would have had to change his economic system, for the sake of an experiment the outcome of which would have been extremely uncertain. It is most unlikely that Upper Palaeolithic or Mesolithic man would ever have been willing to do this.

RESTRICTED NUMBER OF DOMESTICATED SPECIES

The curious fact that, out of an enormous number of available mammalia, only very few have been domesticated has already been mentioned. It is known that others were tried by the

Egyptians and probably similar experiments were made at earlier periods elsewhere. The lake-dwellers of Switzerland, for instance, appear to have domesticated foxes. But as soon as man adopted the Neolithic settled mode of life, restrictions of mobility, space and climate imposed themselves upon him which made it increasingly difficult to try out new species. Moreover, once a sufficient number of species had been domesticated to satisfy the needs of human life, providing man with food and raw material, nothing was to be gained from undertaking the difficult task of reducing additional species to a state of domestication. It is economic considerations as a rule, therefore, that prevent further experiment.

CONCLUSION

To summarize the discussion of this somewhat complex subject it may be helpful to present the results in a concise form. Two sequences have emerged: one comprising the stages of intensity of domestication through which a species would pass in the course of time, and the other being the probable order in which species were domesticated one after the other.

The stages of domestication are as follows:
   a. Loose contacts, with free breeding.
   b. Confinement to human environment, with breeding in captivity.
   c. Selective breeding organized by man, to obtain certain characteristics, and occasional crossing with wild forms.
   d. Economic considerations of man leading to the planned "development" of breeds with certain desirable properties.
   e. Wild ancestors persecuted or exterminated.

The order in which species were taken into domestication is shown in the following list:

1. *Mammals domesticated in the pre-agricultural phase:*
   Dog, reindeer, goat, sheep.
2. *Mammals domesticated in the early agricultural phase:*
   (The crop-robbers. Mainly used for food.)
   Cattle, buffalo, gaur, banteng, yak, pig.
3. *Mammals subsequently domesticated primarily for transport and labour:*
   a. Domesticated by agriculturalists in the forest zone: elephant.
   b. Domesticated by secondary nomads: horse, camel.
   c. Domesticated by river-valley civilizations: ass, onager.
4. *The pest-destroyers:*
   Mongoose, ferret, cat.
5. *Various other mammals:*
   a. The small rodents: rabbit (medieval), dormouse (Roman).
   b. Experimental domestication: hyaena (Egyptian), fox (Neolithic), gazelle (Egyptian), ibex (Egyptian).
   c. New World species: llama (American Indian).
   d. Pets: mouse (modern European).
6. *Birds, fishes, insects* (not classified chronologically).

REFERENCES

Hahn, E. (1896). *Die Haustiere und ihre Beziehungen zur Wirtschaft des Menschen.* Leipzig.

Haskins, C. P. (1945). *Of Ants and Men.* London.

Hatt, G. (1919). "Notes on Reindeer Nomadism." *Mem. Amer. Anthrop. Ass.*, 6: 75–133.

Lane, Y. (1946). *African Folk Tales.* London.

Sirelius, V. T. (1916). "Über die Art und Zeit der Zähmung des Renntiers." *J. Soc. Finno-Ougrienne*, 33 (2).

8.

Animals and Humanitarianism

E. S. Turner

THE ASS FOR BROTHER

One of the major ironies of the eighteenth century was that, as
the laws of England grew progressively more brutal, private
compassion and benevolence expanded.

By 1800 there were two hundred capital offences. Yet, while
aristocrats turned over their thieving valets to the hangman,
while squires caught their tenants in man-traps and had them
shipped to Van Diemen's Land, while tradesmen imprisoned
their pettiest debtors, there were voices ready to demand justice for cocks and cockchafers. The lone humanitarian was liable to be suspected of every aberration from old-fashioned Puri-
tanism to new-fangled Rousseauism or Methodism. He was
dismissed as one suffering from the scourge of "sensibility," that
often morbid obsession with the sufferings of others; and his
seeming unmanly hysteria, his claim to kinship even with creatures that crawled, roused only derision in hardier breasts.

Humanitarianism was not a movement but a state of mind

SOURCE: E. S. Turner, *All Heaven in a Rage* (London: Michael Joseph, Ltd.,
1964; New York: St. Martin's Press, 1965), pp. 65–71, 73–74, 76–77, 81–82,
125–130, 146–148, 229–237. Reprinted by permission of Michael Joseph,
Ltd.

which animated small pockets of the literate world. Its propagandists had no common social, religious or intellectual back-
ground; they included essayists who carried on where Pope and
Addison left off, philanthropists, Romantic poets, novelists of
sensibility, clergymen, utilitarian philosophers, "miscellaneous
writers," the infrequent sportsman, the eccentric and crank,
and the pious, conscience-torn citizen who could not believe
that God had condemned his innocent creatures to misuse and
oblivion.

These propagandists reached the broad road to compassion
by devious routes. Some regarded indulgence to animals as a
natural extension of that spirit of philanthropy which had provided hospitals and foundling homes. Others regarded "rights
for animals" as a natural extension of the "rights of man" and
the "rights of women"; unfortunately, the championing of animals by those who appeared to have absorbed libertarian political notions from France was not always calculated to advance
the cause. Many believed in Hogarth's proposition that cruelty
to animals corrupted those who indulged in it, and were determined to fight it for that reason. Dr. John Hawkesworth said, of
killing for pleasure, that "every practice which, if not criminal
in itself, yet wears out the sympathising sensibility of a tender
mind, must render human nature proportionately less fit for
society."[1] Yet many who believed themselves to be humane
hunted and shot, reserving their censure for the cruelties of
drovers and coachmen. A few took the vegetarian standpoint,
denying that the possession of canine teeth entitled men to eat
meat, and commending the ways of the "tender-hearted Hin-
doo."[2] But Dr. Hawkesworth argued: "If man had lived upon
fruits and herbs the greater part of those animals which died to

1. *Adventurer*, March 13, 1753.
2. See John Oswald's *The Cry of Nature* (1791), the author of which says:
"Vegetation allures our every sense and plays upon the sensorium with a sort
of blandishment which at once flatters and satisfies the soul."

furnish his table would never have lived; instead of increasing the breed as a pledge of plenty he would have been compelled to destroy them to prevent a famine." Dr. Samuel Johnson said as much to Boswell: "There is much talk of the misery which we cause to the brute creation; but they are recompensed by existence. If they were not useful to man and therefore protected by him they would not be nearly so numerous." Boswell wondered whether the beasts which underwent so much for the service and entertainment of man would, if they had the chance, accept existence on those terms.[3] Of Johnson's humanity, there was little question. In the *Idler*, of August 5, 1758, he wrote scathingly of the "race of wretches" who, in the name of physic, cut up dogs alive and, "by familiar cruelty," prepared themselves for that profession which they proposed to exercise on the tender and the helpless; "and if the knowledge of physiology has been somewhat increased, he surely buys knowledge dear who learns the use of the lacteals at the expense of his humanity." The Doctor went out himself to buy oysters for Hodge, his cat, suspecting that if he sent a servant on such a humiliating errand the cat would be the sufferer. He rebuked his wife for chastising the cat in front of the maid, who would thus be able to cite her mistress's example for doing the same.

In the main, compassion for animals was spread by the printed word. Though societies were formed for the suppression of vice, the succouring of small debtors and numerous other purposes, upholders of animals' rights were still too sparse to band together. The literate individual who felt strongly enough about ill-treatment of horses or stoning of cocks could vent his indignation by writing to the *Gentleman's Magazine* or the *Sporting Magazine,* or to the daily newspapers, which were always open to correspondence on such topics. Inevitably, there

3. James Boswell, *Life of Samuel Johnson.*

was much preaching to the converted. "The misfortune is, the writings of an Addison are seldom read by cooks and butchers," lamented a writer in the *World* of August 19, 1756; and that was the measure of the problem. This writer said he had tried to intercede on behalf of ill-treated dogs, cats and sheep but had usually come off worse; moreover, the animals had suffered more grievously as a result of his intercession. "I soon found it necessary to consult my own ease as well as security by turning down another street whenever I met with any adventure of this kind . . ." The usual reaction of an offender, when tackled by a "busybody," was to point out, with oaths if not violence, that the animal was his own, or his master's, and that he was committing no offence in law. Gentlemen hesitated even to reproach their friends for cruelty. "I once attempted to reason with a fellow (and he was of the rich vulgar) who was cruelly beating an innocent horse, till the blood spun from its nostrils," wrote John Lawrence, the sportsman-farmer; "the reply I obtained was, 'G—— d—— my eyes, Jack, you are talking as though the horse was a Christian.' "[4] Occasionally, in the annals of the times, one finds a reference to a vicar who would not allow boys to rob nests, a crank who bought captive birds from boys to set free, a sentimentalist who allowed his old horse to live out its last days in comfort, a woman who succoured stray cats. But examples of this kind were rare and a subject for amused comment.

The spirit of humanitarianism was strengthened by the poets of Nature who took over from the poets of Art. Their contribution cannot be measured in precise terms. The cynic is entitled to point out that, despite a score of odes to the skylark, the world continued to guzzle these birds as never before; but the poets' influence on the collective mind of the nation, down the generations, may have been more potent than anyone sup-

4. *A Philosophical and Practical Treatise on Horses* (1796).

poses. One of the first of the new poets was James Thomson, whose *The Seasons* came out between 1726 and 1730. He notes the fowler engaged in his "falsely cheerful barbarous game of death"; he is unable to admire the valour of men on horseback chasing hares, or even stags. But, in the absence of lions, wolves and boars, there is still one worthy foe—the fox:

> . . . give, ye Britons, then
> Your sportive fury pitiless to pour
> Loose on the nightly robber of the fold . . .

Reynard, whom even Pope describes as "obscene," is to be pursued remorselessly through hedges, ditches and "the shaking wilderness," until he dies hard—

> Without complaint, though by an hundred mouths
> Relentless torn . . .

But Thomson does not care for the sight of pesticide practised by women. He deprecates

> Uncomely courage, unbeseeming skill
> To spring the fence, to reign the prancing steed,
> The cap, the whip, the masculine attire . . .

More passionate in their defence of the brute creation were Burns, Cowper, Blake and Wordsworth. Burns' poem *On Seeing a Hunted Hare which a Fellow Had Just Shot At* begins:

> Inhuman man! curse on thy barbarous art
> And blasted be thy murder-aiming eye;
> May never pity soothe thee with a sigh
> Nor ever pleasure glad thy cruel heart!

A flight of alarmed water fowl fills him with anger at the inhumanity of

> Man, to whom alone is given
> A ray direct from pitying Heaven . . .

and the mouse turned up by the plough finds in the poet a

> . . . poor earth-born companion
> An' fellow mortal.

Cowper, whose Evangelical compassion was nothing if not catholic, wrote poems to, or about, the hare, halibut, cat, spaniel, glow-worm, silkworm, grasshopper, parrot, sparrow, swallow, nightingale, bullfinch, goldfinch and robin. For ten years he kept a tame hare ("one at least is safe") and gave shelter to many other creatures. Field sports revolted him. The huntsman was a boor who took delight in defiling with blood scenes calculated to exalt the mind and compose the passions, a man incapable of feeling for

> The spaniel, dying for some venial fault,
> Under dissection of the knotted scourge.

In *The Task* (1785) Cowper sets out his philosophy in detail:

> I would not enter on my list of friends
> (though graced with polished manners and fine sense
> yet wanting sensibility) the man
> Who needlessly sets foot upon a worm . . .

The poet allows that intruders in man's domain, venomous creatures and "the creeping vermin, loathsome to the sight" may be dispatched; "a necessary act incurs no blame." Man's rights "are paramount and must extinguish theirs." But, as a broad principle,

> . . . they are all—the meanest things that are—
> As free to live and to enjoy that life
> As God was free to form them at the first . . .

For all his advanced sensibility Cowper was no vegetarian:

> Feed them, and yield
> Thanks for the food. Carnivorous thro' sin,

Feed on the slain, but spare the living brute.

The poet yielded thanks for his food, not only to God, but to various good ladies who sent him presents of game, fish and oysters (the oyster was a "living brute" but Cowper did not see fit to spare him). Some might feel that his lines to the halibut, a fish never before and perhaps never since apostrophised, lacked the humanitarian fire of some of the others:

> Thy lot thy brethren of the slimy fin
> Would envy could they know that thou wast doom'd
> To feed a bard and be addressed in verse.

Blake's compassion was confused with mysticism, but even the simplest minds could get the message of

> A robin redbreast in a cage
> Puts all heaven in a rage.
> A dove-house filled with doves and pigeons
> Shudders Hell through all its regions.
> A dog starved at his master's gate
> Predicts the ruin of the state.
> A horse misused upon the road
> Calls to Heaven for human blood.
> Each outcry of the hunted hare
> A fibre from the brain does tear.
> A skylark wounded in the wing,
> A cherubim does cease to sing.
> The game cock clipped and armed for fight
> Does the rising sun affright . . .

If Burns was ready to claim kinship with the mouse, Blake claimed it with the fly:

> Am not I
> A fly like thee?
> Or art not thou
> A man like me?
> For I dance

And drink and sing
Till some blind hand
Shall brush my wing.

Those to whom such verses were the ravings of sick minds enjoyed a coarse laugh when Coleridge, in the *Morning Chronicle* in 1794, wrote a "Poem to a Young Ass" containing the words "I hail thee *Brother.*" . . .

Yet, before the century's end, humanitarians were ready to risk a multiplication of taunts by demanding legal rights for animals. Jeremy Bentham, the political philosopher, did so in his *Introduction to the Principles of Morals and Legislation* (printed 1780, published 1789). Utilitarianism, of which Bentham was the chief exponent, stood for the greatest happiness of the greatest number; and that greatest number, in Bentham's view, included animals. He complained of the long neglect beasts had suffered at the hands of jurists, who had degraded them into the class of things, and said: "The day *may* come, when the rest of the animal creation may acquire those rights which never could have been withholden from them but by the hand of tyranny." Men might yet recognise that "the number of the legs, the villosity of the skin, or the termination of the *os sacrum,*" were reasons insufficient for abandoning a sensitive being to torture. "What else is it that should trace the insuperable line? Is it the faculty of reason, or, perhaps, the faculty of discourse? But a full-grown horse or dog is beyond comparison a more rational, as well as a more conversable animal, than an infant of a day, or a week, or even a month, old. But suppose the case were otherwise, what would it avail? The question is not, Can they *reason?* nor, Can they *talk?* but, Can they *Suffer?*" In his *Principles of Penal Law* Bentham asked: "Why should the law refuse its protection to any sensitive being? The time will come when humanity will extend its mantle over everything which breathes." . . .

MRS. TRIMMER TAKES A HAND

How, in a brutal world, were children to be schooled in compassion towards animals? How was the new benevolence which filled the philosophers to be instilled in those who saw their elders lashing horses and stoning cocks? "Pity is not natural to men," said Dr. Johnson. "Children are always cruel. Savages are always cruel. Pity is acquired and improved by the cultivation of reason."[5] Pope, as we have seen, thought "a very good use" might be made of the fancy which children felt for birds and animals, but how was that fancy to be controlled and directed? Animal stories of the type on which children are nurtured today did not exist. Most of the "Mother Goose" nursery rhymes taught to children were cheerfully heartless fancies in which the cow with the crumpled horn tossed the dog that worried the cat that killed the rat that ate the malt; the world of the little man who had a little gun, of cats down the well, of mice docked by carving knives, of blackbirds baked in pies. It is improbable that these rhymes, of themselves, fostered cruelty to animals, but few of them were calculated to rouse kindness. Even the better-intentioned rhymes probably misfired. "Has any child ever felt any real sympathy towards Mother Hubbard's dog?" asked Miss Victoria Sackville-West. The average child, she thought, would be more likely to regard the dog's disappointment as an excellent practical joke.[6]

In the last quarter of the eighteenth century a handful of authors, rising to Pope's challenge, tackled the task of rousing sympathy for animals in the breasts of older children. Their writings are, to our taste, sententious, mawkish, equivocal and

5. Boswell, *Life of Samuel Johnson.*
6. *Nursery Rhymes.*

often ridiculous, but they became "required reading" in innumerable homes. Many of them were reprinted over and over again, sometimes down to our own times; and their influence on Victorian middle-class attitudes may well have been considerable. Among notable writers in this class were Dr. Thomas Percival, Mrs. Ann Letitia Barbauld, Mrs. Sarah Trimmer, Thomas Day and Mary Wollstonecraft. . . .

One of the most enduring of these didactic works was *The History of Sandford and Merton,* by Thomas Day, of whom it was said that his many eccentricities were but symptoms of his nobility of character. Even as a boy at Charterhouse, he went out of his way to be compassionate to animals. When Sir William Jones said to him: "Day, kill that spider," the boy replied: "No, I don't know that I have a right. Suppose that a superior being said to a companion, 'Kill that lawyer,' how should you like it? And a lawyer is more noxious to most people than a spider."[7]

Sandford and Merton appeared in three volumes between 1783 and 1789. Harry Sandford, son of a plain honest farmer, does not steal eggs or torment animals, and is careful to step out of the way of worms, a course of behaviour which makes him "a great favourite with everybody." Less fastidious is Tommy Merton, a rich man's son, but Harry's influence redeems him. Harry's first big test comes when he sees a hunted hare limping past and resolves not to tell the huntsmen which way it went. The leading rider is the squire who lashes Harry with his whip when the information is not forthcoming. "Now! you little rascal, do you choose to tell me now?" demands the horseman, and Harry says: "If I would not tell you before I won't now, though you should kill me." Another rider comes up and remonstrates with the aggressor: "It is an happy day for you, squire, that his age is not equal to his spirit. But you are always passionate . . ." Just then the hounds recover the scent and the hunt

7. *Dictionary of National Biography.*

gallops off, leaving Harry to boast that his ordeal was nothing compared to what the young Spartans had to suffer. In due course Harry saves the life of the squire, who is being dragged by his horse, and is offered a guinea. "Harry with a look of more contempt than he had ever been seen to assume before rejected the present."

The boys then hear of an impending bull-baiting. Harry tries to persuade his companions that they should not go to watch this cruel and dangerous spectacle, "particularly Master Merton, whose mother loves him so much and is so careful about him." This advice is "not received with approbation." When the bull breaks loose, rushing "like lightning over the plain," it is Harry who with a pitchfork, saves Tommy from being gored; his own life is then saved by a young Negro whom he earlier rescued from bullying.

It is not too much to say that the author of *Sandford and Merton* was killed by kindness. In 1789 he set off on an unbroken colt to visit his wife and mother at Bear Hill, convinced that any animal could be controlled by gentle means. Near Wargrove the colt shied and threw him on his head, with fatal results.

Mary Wollstonecraft's *Original Stories* (1788) were modelled on those of Mrs. Trimmer. Mary and Caroline, children of wealthy parents who have allowed servants to fill them with every kind of vulgar prejudice, are taken in hand by Mrs. Mason. Seeing her walk in wet grass rather than tread on insects, they ask why she does not kill them, and receive the reply: "You are often troublesome—I am stronger than you—yet I do not kill you." When a boy shoots a lark and badly injures it, Mrs. Mason bravely puts her foot on its head, "turning her own another way." Eagerly the children enquire how they should behave to prove that they are superior to animals, and Mrs. Mason says: "Be tender-hearted . . . it is only to animals that children *can* do good. Men are their superiors." . . .

THE WILBERFORCE OF HACKS

The man who, eventually, picked up the torch which had burned Lord Erskine's fingers was the voluble, erratic Member of Parliament for Galway, Richard Martin ("Humanity" Martin). He had supported Sir William Pulteney's Bill in 1800 but not until he was in his late sixties did he start to badger Parliament with his long series of measures on behalf of animals. Born to wealth, Martin played the benevolent despot in Connemara, of which he owned 200,000 acres. From the door of his castle at Ballynahinch he could drive thirty miles before he reached his gatehouse. Here he was "unapproachable by legal process" and was said to have driven off a process-server with a blunderbuss. It is noteworthy that he was a keen follower of field sports; many of his pronouncements would shock the anti-hunting propagandist of today. Like any Irish gentleman he was jealous of his honour. In his day he duelled with the notorious "Fighting Fitzgerald" and had the scars of several pistol shots on his body. William Jerdan, the memoirist, who was privileged to see these scars, said that Martin "appeared to value human life at a lower estimate than the life of a dog or an ass," qualifying this somewhat by adding: "Dick Martin might have a gentle regard for bipeds as well as quadrupeds; but it was his special vocation to protect and preserve the latter and to care surprisingly little for the former who, he thought, might take care of themselves."[8] However, in the same year—1821—that he introduced his first Ill-Treatment of Horses Bill, Martin spoke vigorously in Parliament against the death penalty for forgery. He asked the Solicitor-General to consider what advice he would give to his ward at a university if a friend of that ward committed a forgery at

8. *Men I Have Known.*

his expense for £50 or £100. Surely the only advice was: "If you wish to live happily in college, do not hang your friend or companion. Forfeit your recognizance to prosecute if you have entered into one, for no young lady of rank and fortune will ever marry a man who has hanged his friend and companion." Martin said he knew many who had prosecuted for forgery and would lament it until they died.

The Member for Galway was not too well received by the Parliamentary reporters of his day and he clashed repeatedly with *The Times* and the *Morning Post* ("Sir, did I ever spake in italics?" he demanded of the *Morning Post* editor). At Westminster he enjoyed the reputation of a "character." He was passionate and garrulous, sincere and humorous. Nobody took him too seriously, yet nobody underestimated him. Once, when cries of "Hare! Hare!" interrupted him, he crossed the floor of the House to the place whence the sounds came and with "infinite mildness" asked who had uttered them. No one answered, but someone pointed slyly to a City Member. "Oh, it was only an alderman!" said Martin, turning on his heel and resuming his place. The House thought it a good joke.[9] It is probable that a pedant could never have gained the support of Parliament for a cause which many believed to be essentially ludicrous.

When he moved his Ill-Treatment of Horses Bill, Martin told a curious story against himself (*The Times* reported it, but *Hansard* left it out). He said he had seen a man abusing a horse on Ludgate Hill and had been strongly tempted to chastise him personally, but instead he paid two men five shillings to do so. Later he had inadvertently repeated this story in the hearing of the victim, who then summoned him for assault at Bow Street. The magistrate advised Martin to compromise by paying the victim £5, which he did.

Several Members who regarded the Bill as meddling legisla-

9. William Jerdan, *Men I Have Known.*

tion gave Martin credit for his motives. But when Alderman C. Smith suggested that protection should be given to asses, there were such howls of laughter that *The Times* reporter could hear little of what was said. When the chairman repeated this proposal, the laughter was intensified. Another Member said Martin would be legislating for dogs next, which caused a further roar of mirth, and a cry "And cats!" sent the House into convulsions. Despite all this, the Commons accepted the Bill. What happened to it in the Lords, *Hansard* does not say, but at some stage it was lost.

In the following year Martin widened the scope of his Bill to include cattle and tried again. The Attorney-General, Sir Robert Gifford, opposed it and was told by its originator that he had "placed himself in opposition to the common-sense of the whole nation." Every preacher in London, he said, had spoken in support of the Bill. He made it clear that he would not object to a stubborn horse being beaten; but his object was to protect it from inhumane treatment. A Member complained that, as a magistrate, he would not know how to act if a post-boy were brought before him for over-riding a horse. Another Member foresaw laws to prevent the boiling of lobsters and the eating of live oysters. But this time both Houses passed the Bill, the task of steering it through the Lords being performed, appropriately, by Lord Erskine. It was now an offence wantonly and cruelly to "beat, abuse, or ill-treat any horse, mare, gelding, mule, ass, ox, cow, heifer, steer, sheep or other cattle." Parliament had refused to include the word "bull." A fine of 10s was the minimum penalty and the maximum was two months' imprisonment. The day on which this historic measure received the Royal assent was June 22, 1822.

To pass the Bill was one thing; to enforce it was another. The magistracy of England were less enthusiastic about the Act than its sponsor. With the object of ensuring that it should not become a dead letter, Richard Martin went about London gather-

158   E. S. TURNER

ing evidence against cruel carters, drovers and coachmen, on whom he caused summonses to be served. Legend has it that in one of his first cases he led a maltreated donkey into court, but legend almost certainly lies. Whatever incident inspired this tale also inspired the song which contains the lines:

> If I had a donkey wot wouldn't go,
> D'you think I'd wollop him? No, no, no!
> I'd give him some hay and cry 'Gee-ho!'

Perhaps the first case brought by Martin was at the Guildhall, on August 11, 1822. He had asked *The Times* not to report his Parliamentary speeches, since its accounts did not show him in a favourable light, but the newspaper said it would not, presumably, incur his displeasure by reporting the court proceedings. On this occasion Martin prosecuted Samuel Clarke and David Hyde for savagely beating tethered horses at Smithfield. Clarke explained that his horse was standing "very sleepy and dull," and he admitted hitting it a few times to make it show a little life and spirit. Hyde had belaboured his horse with the butt of a whip whenever it held its head at an angle other than that which he approved. When Hyde said he was a butcher by trade, Martin interjected: "Yes, I perceive that. A horse butcher." Beatings like these were an old Smithfield custom, designed to make horses look more marketable. The men were fined 20s each.

Sometimes Martin paid the fines himself, taking no pleasure in punishing employees rather than employers. His appearances were often a profound embarrassment to the magistrates, for he was intolerant of the bland ways of the Bar and did not modify his language. In Connemara he had been accustomed, as sole magistrate, to clap offenders in his own lake isle lock-up. He will be seen at his most truculent in the next chapter; but it is fair to say that Martin's court appearances alone would have earned him Thomas Hood's tribute:

Thou Wilberforce of hacks!
Of whites as well as blacks,
Piebald and dapple grey,
Chestnut and bay—
No poet's eulogy thy name adorns!
But oxen, from the fens,
Sheep, in their pens,
Praise thee, and red cows with their winding horns!

Martin's friend, John Lawrence, whom he consulted before drafting his famous Act, wrote of him in 1825: "The name of Martin of Galway will wear well; it will live in our annals and attract posterity as a symbol of blessed compassion, where it is most needed . . . he has actually worked an incipient and beneficial change in the character of the London rabble. He has not only worked upon their fears but he has even taught them to think! And this he has effected without the usual consequences —loss of popularity."[10]

Yet it required more than Martin to enforce "Martin's Act." In August of 1822 a company of humanitarians met in Old Slaughter's Coffee-House, St. Martin's Lane, London, under the chairmanship of the Rev. Arthur Broome, to consider forming a society to protect animals—some fourteen years after Liverpool had pointed the way. The session at Old Slaughter's was unproductive; but another was held in 1824, with Fowell (later Sir Fowell) Buxton, MP, in the chair, and the result was the founding of the (now Royal) Society for the Prevention of Cruelty to Animals. It is noteworthy that Buxton and William Wilberforce, another founder member, were both leaders in the fight against Negro slavery. Three other Members of Parliament, one of them Richard Martin, lent their support and so did three clergymen. Broome, vicar of the church now called St. Mary's, Bromley-by-Bow, undertook the secretaryship. At his

10. *Sporting Magazine,* May, 1825.

own expense he had already employed a man named Wheeler to gather evidence of abuses.[11] Although resources were meagre, severely limiting the diffusion of literature, the Society became a force to be reckoned with in the area around Smithfield. In its first year it brought nearly 150 prosecutions. . . .

CHALLENGE TO THE RSPCA

In 1840 the Society for the Prevention of Cruelty to Animals acquired the prefix "Royal" (in that year a Society was also founded in Scotland). The young Victoria had become a patron before her accession and continued to take a personal interest throughout her reign; though some of her activities, like her repeated visits to Van Amburgh's animal shows, must have caused the Society some embarrassment. From roughly this period the RSPCA began to lay more stress on education and propaganda, not wishing to be known purely as a prosecuting society. In 1841 it decided not to accept any money awarded by the courts but to divert such sums to charity. To punish carters for cruelty might be necessary; to reward kindly carters with medals seemed a better idea. To watch for cruelty on Ludgate Hill might also be necessary, but why not provide help there? As it turned out, the provision of trace horses on notorious inclines was not such a good idea, as carters grossly overloaded their carts in the knowledge that they would receive assistance.[12]

The task of educating children to kindness was a little easier than it had been in Mrs. Trimmer's day, though adults still set plenty of dubious examples. New and less heartless nursery rhymes were beginning to appear, among them "Mary Had a

11. Arthur W. Moss, *Valiant Crusade* (1961).
12. E. G. Fairholme and Wellesley Pain, *A Century of Work for Animals* (1924).

Little Lamb," published in 1830 by Mrs. Sarah Josepha Hale, of Boston, USA. Its last verse was frankly propagandist:

> Why does the lamb love Mary so?
>   The eager children cry;
> Why, Mary loves the lamb, you know,
>   The teacher did reply.

About ten years later "I Love Little Pussy," made its appearance, with this as its smug last verse:

> She shall sit by my side,
>   And I'll give her some food;
> And pussy will love me
>   Because I am good.[13]

Handbooks for governesses and nursemaids laid down that all tendency towards cruelty by the young must be firmly discouraged; not even a beetle was to be crushed in a child's presence. To indoctrinate older children, the RSPCA began to distribute tracts, to give lectures and to hold prize essay competitions. Their efforts were not eased by the circulation of such manuals as the *Boy's Own Book*, first published in 1828. Wrote the anonymous compiler: "Whether the boy catches his sparrow in the common brick trap, ensnares a linnet to the lime twig, secures a score of larks or finches with the clap net, or takes a nest of full-fledged blackbirds, he experiences a gratification which we have often felt but cannot now describe." There were instructions for breaking birds to captivity. A boy who kept pouter pigeons was warned that if a bird became gorged it would be necessary to "slit the crop from the bottom, take out the meat, wash the crop and sew it up again." Some of the amusements listed err on the side of impracticability; as, for instance, the "Flying Egg," consisting of a goose egg broken open, its contents replaced by a live bat, and the halves glued

13. Iona and Peter Opie, *The Oxford Dictionary of Nursery Rhymes* (1951).

together again. The lesson of this book was that Nature was there for a boy's "gratification"; that, and no more.

Not all supporters of the RSPCA were convinced that it was possible to make people humane by Act of Parliament. Vices, they said, would die out in a world being warmed with benevolence. If action was needed, it should be directed towards increasing the growth of that benevolence. These arguments were heard in many other contexts; they were a justification for taking no action against sweeps who pushed boys up chimneys. In fact, legislation in the nineteenth century did much to make people humane, if only by making inhumanity dangerous and unprofitable. . . .

RSPCA FORGES ON

In its educational role, the Society was active on many fronts. Not its least success in the 1860s was to persuade clergymen to hold an Animal Sunday, the example being set by Dean Stanley, Dean of Westminster. A great propaganda campaign, involving meetings and demonstrations, was concentrated on carters, drivers and coachmen; those who could read were given handbooks on the care of the horse. But the cruelties which horses underwent were not caused by their drivers alone. The Society agitated against the practice of "paving" roads with sharp flints and leaving the horses to tread them down; also against the operation of brakeless omnibuses, the animals being expected to stop or slow the vehicle by muscle-power. A long-standing reproach was remedied—in London at least—by the installation of drinking-troughs for horses and cattle. The body responsible had begun by providing fountains for human beings, but in 1867 it became the Metropolitan Free Drinking Fountain and Cattle Trough Association.

To reward conscientious workers for the cause, the Society

introduced a Queen's Medal, John Colam being its first recipient. The initial design for this award had featured a variety of domestic creatures, but not a cat. Queen Victoria detected the omission and drew in a cat with her own hand, being anxious that everything should be done to abate the prejudice against this creature.[14] The Society offered prizes for improved methods of killing, notably in the shape of more humane traps and snares for rabbits.

In 1870 for the first time women began to take a directing hand in the affairs of the RSPCA. The Ladies' Committee formed in that year was founded by Miss Angela (a year later, Baroness) Burdett-Coutts, following a suggestion by George Angell, the American humanitarian. The Baroness was one of the Great Victorians and well deserves her tomb in Westminster Abbey. A daughter of Sir Francis Burdett, she added the name Coutts in 1837 when the major share in Coutts' Bank was left to her. As the richest heiress in England she drew much attention at the Coronation of Queen Victoria, of whom she was a close life-long friend. Declining all early suitors, she administered her own fortune, supporting almost every philanthropic cause from ragged schools and the housing of the poor to female emigration and the Flower Girls Brigade. It was said of her that "no other woman under the rank of Queen ever did so much for the Established Church."[15] To the RSPCA her tall, serene, black figure brought enormous prestige, and its Ladies' Committee became a body of great strength and influence.

The Committee concentrated on propaganda, in schools, in the press and among carters and drovers, who now received their good conduct awards direct from the Baroness. One driver who was sacked because he refused to commit an act of cruelty was presented with a bound volume of *Animal World*

14. Fairholme and Pain, *A Century of Work for Animals.*
15. *Dictionary of National Biography.*

and, one hopes, another job. In 1885 the Baroness and Sir Walter Gilbey inaugurated London's annual cart-horse parade, which became so popular that entries had to be limited to one thousand.

It was a Victorian belief that essay-writing, if not ennobling in itself, helped in the clarification and strengthening of ideas. Carters and drovers could not be set to this task, but schoolchildren could. In a short space the prize essay contests started by the Ladies' Committee achieved a popularity hard to credit in this sophisticated day. By 1889 one thousand schools were competing, to the tune of 40,000 essays. It became a task for royalty to present the prizes at such centres as the Crystal Palace, the Albert Hall or Alexandra Palace, which were the scenes of gigantic, but always decorous, beanos. Even in the twentieth century the essay competitions continued to gather momentum; the total submitted by London schools alone in the RSPCA's jubilee year verged on the quarter-million.[16]

Soon after the Ladies' Committee was formed, the idea was conceived of recruiting the young into a humanitarian movement of their own. The temperance reformers had already shown the way; since the 1840s there had been Bands of Hope, the young members of which pledged themselves never to touch drink. Why not similar groups of youngsters pledged never to harm animals? In the 'seventies the first Bands of Mercy[17] began to appear. The credit for originating this movement is generally given to Mrs. Catherine Smithies, of Wood Green, whose husband helped to found *Animal World*. Soon Bands of Mercy were being formed in the Dominions and in America and by 1883 the organisation was formally linked with the RSPCA. The children listened to readings and lectures; they sang "All things bright and beautiful"; they learned innumera-

16. Fairholme and Pain, *A Century of Work for Animals*.
17. Now the Animal Defenders movement.

ble poems with names like "Dobbin's Friend," "Hide, Birdie, Hide," "Jessie to her Dead Robin," "Don't Rob the Birds of Their Eggs, Boys," "Only a Cur" and "Boys Don't Throw Stones"; they took part in tableaux and parades, each member carrying one of the letters which spelled out "A Band of Mercy"; and they qualified for medals. Mostly the organisation was run by women, but clergymen and even squires were co-opted to deliver readings. Mrs. Florence Suckling, an active pioneer of the movement, outlined numerous exercises for Bands of Mercy in her book, *The Humane Educator*. There was a play which began with Mrs. Percy rebuking some young girls for gushing over a hat with a bird on it. Sarah Jane, the maid, was so ashamed that she decided to empty a water jug down the gun of Mr. Quickshot, the pigeon-shooter, and dip all his cartridges in warm water. The barrels burst in his face. The girls told him that 13,848 goldfinches were sent to London from Worthing in a single year and that a pair of sparrows in one week could destroy 4,000 caterpillars. Alice suggests that if Mr. Quickshot really must shoot he should join the Rifle Volunteers; and Mr. Quickshot had the grace to admit that there was force in their arguments. When Sarah suggested that hats could be trimmed with artificial birds, Mrs. Percy exclaimed, "My dear, the idea is as bad as the act!" It seems improbable that plays like this had any effect on the Mr. Quickshots of real life; but they may have helped to bring up a new generation with a distaste for "murderous millinery."

The Band of Mercy movement spread many legends about faithful animals, the most famous of these being Greyfriars Bobby. In 1858 a labourer called Gray died and was buried in Greyfriars Churchyard, Edinburgh. Afterwards his dog was found on his grave and, though often dislodged, always came back. A restaurant-keeper fed him every day. The Lord Provost exempted Bobby from the dog tax and gave him a collar inscribed: "Greyfriars Bobby. Presented to him by the Lord Provost of Edinburgh, 1867." When the dog died in 1872 the curator of the churchyard found him a grave near his master. Finally a fountain was raised in Bobby's honour by Baroness Burdett-Coutts.

It was an unusual lantern lecture which did not feature a picture of Greyfriars Bobby. Other slides might show "Old Shepherd's Chief Mourner" (also a dog) or "Alpine Mastiffs reanimating a Distressed Traveller" or similar works by Landseer; perhaps pictures of Cowper and his hares, or the Earl of Shaftesbury or even the Duke of Wellington. The Duke was a Band of Mercy hero because of the way he befriended a boy whom he found crying over a tame toad. No one, the boy explained, was willing to look after his pet when he went to boarding-school, so the Duke undertook to do so. He sent five letters to the boy reporting on the toad's welfare, one of them reading:

"Field-Marshal the Duke of Wellington is happy to inform William Harris that his toad is alive and well."

Strathfieldsaye, July 27, 1837.

When the boy returned for his Christmas holidays, his pet was safely enjoying its winter sleep.[18]

No soldier had a better claim to figure in this gallery of honour than Sir Charles Napier. In the fierce Indian heat, while men died round him from apoplexy, he shared his tent with his charger, Red Rover. Angrily he fought against the over-loading of baggage camels, which were supposed to carry no more than 350 pounds. "Yet I have seized and weighed the loads of many camels on the march which have passed 8,000 pounds," he wrote.[19]

It had long been a taunt, though seldom a deserved one, that persons who were eager to prevent cruelty to animals did not

18. Florence Suckling, *The Humane Educator*.
19. Rosamund Lawrence, *Charles Napier*.

care about cruelty to children. In 1884, in curious circumstances, the RSPCA helped to form the National Society for the
Prevention of Cruelty to Children. In New York, Henry Bergh,
pioneer of America's animal welfare societies, was asked to
intercede on behalf of "a little animal" suffering at the hands of
a brutal woman. The little animal turned out to be a child.
Bergh rose to the challenge and successfully prosecuted the
woman for cruelty to an animal. After this many similar cases
were brought and a special society was formed in New York to
protect children. The RSPCA, informed of these events, decided that a similar organisation ought to be started in Britain
and the necessary steps were taken by Lord Shaftesbury and
the Rev. Benjamin Waugh.[20]

It is unlikely that the English courts, which had ruled that
bulls were not cattle, would have decided that children were
animals.

In the propaganda field, a new campaigning body began to
assert itself from 1891 onwards: the Humanitarian League. Its
object was to advocate humane principles from a strictly rational standpoint. The League was founded by Henry Salt, Ernest Bell, the publisher, and others and remained active until
1919. While humanity to animals was perhaps its major preoc-
cupation, it was concerned also with prison reform, the aboli-
tion of corporal and capital punishment, workshop sweating
and so on. Salt, a former master of Eton College, kept open
house for Fabians, rationalists, reformers, mystics and intellectuals of all stamps, a frequent visitor being George Bernard
Shaw ("we were Shelleyans and Humanitarians," the play-
wright wrote). According to Stephen Winsten,[21] Salt was anxious that the League should not become a depository for senti-

20. A. W. Moss, *Valiant Crusade.*
21. *Salt and His Circle.*

mental indulgences and false enthusiasms, and this is evident from the general tone of the *Humane Review*, the League's organ. The reviewer of Florence Suckling's *Humane Educator* complained strongly that "the treatment of animals in verse has been almost as bad as their treatment in actual life." He quoted Martin Tupper's appeal to boys to be kind to beasts:

I wot your lot is somewhat rough,
  But theirs is somewhat rougher;
No hopes, no love, but pain enough,
  And only sense to suffer;
You men and boys have friends and joys,
  And homes and hopes in measure—
But these poor brutes are only mutes,
  And never knew a pleasure.

"It would be impossible," wrote the reviewer, "to cram into eight lines a more appalling concentration of good intentions, bad poetry and worse thought." To hedge off animals as dumb and senseless, he said, was to ensure that they would be treated accordingly. He much preferred "the great, breezy, healthful utterance of Whitman":

I think I could turn and live with animals, they're so placid and self-contained,
  I stand and look at them long and long.
They do not sweat and whine about their condition,
They do not lie awake in the dark and weep for their sins,
They do not make me sick discussing their duty to God,
Not one is dissatisfied, not one is demented with the mania of owning things,
Not one kneels to another, nor to his kind that lived thousands of years ago.
Not one is respectable or unhappy over the whole earth.[22]

22. *Song of Myself* (1855).

Though its approach was primarily intellectual, the League was ready to lodge protests and send deputations, as for example when three of its members called on the Shechita Board to protest at Jewish methods of slaughter. And it did not spurn the emotional aid of Lady Florence Dixie, a one-time "female Nimrod" anxious to atone for the deer whose throats she had cut.

A feature of the century was the tendency of the naturalist to become an observer—and later a photographer—rather than a killer. For too long Nature had been studied in the stuffed trophy. Richard Jefferies, Henry Thoreau and Ernest Thompson Seton were among those who set the new fashion. Each began by killing the creatures he loved, but—like Sir Edwin Landseer lining up a stag—found it harder and harder to pull the trigger. Thoreau's advocacy of sitting and watching wild creatures inspired a certain amount of derision. Asked by the puzzled people of Concord why he did not shoot a bird if he wanted to study it, he replied, "Do you think I should shoot you if I wanted to study you?" In *Walden* he wrote that of late years he had found he could not fish without falling a little in self-respect. He helped to shoot a moose but the operation was "too much like going out at night to some woodside pasture and shooting your neighbour's horses."

In their writings and sketch-books the new race of naturalists roused the curiosity of new generations in *living* creatures. Nature books for the young became an industry. Boys' papers dropped their articles on home taxidermy and gave instructions in nature photography instead. Not all the new writers represented animals behaving as animals and many of their works were blatantly sentimental, or anthropomorphic; but the general result was to spread affection and respect for wild creatures.

73 74 75   12 11 10 9 8 7 6 5 4 3 2 1